WALKI

CALD

Paul Hannon

HILLSIDE

HILLSIDE GUIDES - ACROSS THE NORTH

Long Distance Walks
- •THE COAST TO COAST WALK
- •DALES WAY COMPANION
- •THE WESTMORLAND WAY
- •NORTH BOWLAND TRAVERSE
- •FURNESS WAY
- •CLEVELAND WAY COMPANION
- •THE CUMBERLAND WAY
- •LADY ANNE'S WAY

Circular Walks - Lancashire
- •BOWLAND
- •PENDLE & THE RIBBLE

Circular Walks - Yorkshire Dales
- •HOWGILL FELLS
- •THREE PEAKS
- •MALHAMDALE
- •WHARFEDALE
- •NIDDERDALE
- •WENSLEYDALE
- •SWALEDALE

Circular Walks - North York Moors
- •BOOK ONE - WESTERN MOORS
- •BOOK TWO - SOUTHERN MOORS
- •BOOK THREE - NORTHERN MOORS

Circular Walks - South Pennines
- •BRONTE COUNTRY
- •CALDERDALE
- •ILKLEY MOOR

Circular Walks - North Pennines
- •TEESDALE
- •EDEN VALLEY

Hillwalking - Lake District
- •OVER LAKELAND MOUNTAINS
- •OVER LAKELAND FELLS

Yorkshire Pub Walks
- •HARROGATE/WHARFE VALLEY
- •HAWORTH/AIRE VALLEY

Large format colour hardback

FREEDOM OF THE DALES

BIKING COUNTRY
- •YORKSHIRE DALES CYCLE WAY
- •WEST YORKSHIRE CYCLE WAY
- •MOUNTAIN BIKING - WEST & SOUTH YORKSHIRE
- •AIRE VALLEY BIKING GUIDE
- •CALDERDALE BIKING GUIDE

- •WALKING COUNTRY TRIVIA QUIZ
Over 1000 questions on the great outdoors

Send a S.A.E. for a detailed catalogue and pricelist

WALKING COUNTRY

CALDERDALE

Paul Hannon

HILLSIDE

HILLSIDE
PUBLICATIONS
11 Nessfield Grove
Keighley
West Yorkshire
BD22 6NU

First published in 1989 in different format
as *Walks in Calderdale*
This fully revised and extended 3rd edition
first published1996

© Paul Hannon 1989,1996

ISBN 1 870141 44 X

Cover illustration:
Stoodley Pike from above Lumbutts
Back cover: Hardcastle Crags; Warland;
Crimsworth Dean; Midgley Moor
(Paul Hannon/Big Country Picture Library)

Page 1: Churn Milk Joan, Midgley Moor
Page 3: Oxygrains Old Bridge, Booth Dean

Printed in Great Britain by
Carnmor Print and Design
95-97 London Road
Preston
Lancashire
PR1 4BA

CONTENTS

INTRODUCTION

South Pennines is the generally accepted term for that part of the Pennine range lying between the Yorkshire Dales and the Peak District, and the area explored in these pages constitutes the very heart of this area, the upper valley of Yorkshire's river Calder. This is an extremely well defined and compact geographical unit, the moorland watersheds with neighbouring valleys in Yorkshire and Lancashire being the limit of exploration. Only to the east, where the Calder leaves the high country for the larger industrial towns, must an arbitrary line be drawn. Since 1974 the title *Calderdale* has been put to use in local government, with whose patch we coincide apart from the aforementioned lower third of the district, where the conurbations of Halifax, Sowerby Bridge, Brighouse and Elland are found.

This guide commences at the 'gateway' of Sowerby Bridge, where the district's two rivers, Calder and Ryburn, merge. Upstream the Ryburn Valley strikes south to Ripponden and the moors, while the main valley heads west to the upper dale's two towns of Hebden Bridge and Todmorden. On the way it absorbs major side valleys carved out by Luddenden Brook, Cragg Brook, Hebden Water and Walsden Water.

The larger settlements squeeze into the cramped valley floor, shared with river, canal, road and railway. Steep flanks rise to intervening ledges where older villages, predecessors of their bigger brothers below, almost shake hands across deep divides. Higher still, rough pasture gives way to open moorland, where the mill chimney 2 miles away might as well be 200 miles distant. Calderdale's beauty is its unique blend of town and country: here the two are inextricably linked, and once one accepts less appealing aspects of modern industry, then one can revel in a feast of fascinating walking.

Heptonstall old church

Many features of this district's industrial past, in particular, provide much of interest to the observant walker. The hills hereabouts are laced with a centuries old network of trading routes used mainly by packhorses: many of these escaped 'improvement', and numerous sections of stone causeway have survived, laying virtually dormant in wait for today's foot-traveller to bring them back to life, albeit for a new purpose. Hugging the valley bottom, in contrast, is the Rochdale Canal, which largely replaced the packhorse routes and whose towpath now provides miles of leisurely, uninterrupted walking.

Tumbling to the floor of the upper dale at regular intervals are short lived but deep-cut and richly wooded little valleys; these are cloughs, where some of the earliest mills were built in the most unlikely settings. Up on the tops one is never far from a reservoir, the earlier ones made to serve the canal, others to slake the ever-growing thirsts of the towns down the valley. This is definitive gritstone country, and sharing the higher ground with the reservoirs are numerous clusters of boulders and crags, the weathered natural outcrops outshining the countless sites of former quarries. Mainly small-scale operations known as 'delphs', they provided material for the hoary drystone walls, reservoirs and buildings throughout the dale.

Interestingly enough the river Calder, underlying theme of these walks, is seen very infrequently, and its bank is certainly never followed. Occasional spells by the canal do give us rare opportunities to encounter it, but by accident rather than design. No, Calderdale's walking is not in the valley bottom, it is to be found on the hillsides and bracing tops of this characterful upland. A particularly welcome aspect of walking in this well populated district is the availability of public transport - see overleaf.

7

The good waymarking and condition of paths is an indication of the local authority's commendable valuation of its outstanding footpath network. In our travels we encounter the Pennine Way, which crosses the area from Blackstone Edge in the south to Walshaw Dean in the north; and the Calderdale Way, a 50-mile path encircling the district. The latter is a fine example of what can be achieved in an 'unfashionable' area, and its popularity is a fitting tribute to the work involved in its creation. This too we encounter, on numerous occasions.

Getting around

The area is normally approached from Halifax, which has good bus and train links with points further afield. The main bus service, as well as the trains, runs along the dale floor from Halifax to Todmorden. With a little planning, any number of permutations can be created by linking different sections of the walks, to create longer routes or to take advantage of public transport. Most starting points are served by bus, and over half of the walks are within two miles of a railway station.

Using the guide

Each walk is self-contained, with essential information being followed by a simple map and concise description of the route. Dovetailed between this are useful notes of features along the way, and interspersed are illustrations which both capture the flavour of the walks and document the many items of interest. Please remember to obey legitimate signs encountered on your walks: rights of way can be opened, closed or diverted. On these occasions the official notices should take precedence over the guidebook.

The simple sketch maps identify the location of the routes rather than the fine detail, and whilst the route description should be sufficient to guide you around, an Ordnance Survey map is recommended. The route as depicted can easily be plotted on the relevant OS map. To gain the most from a walk, the remarkable detail of the 1:25,000 scale maps cannot be matched: they also serve to vary walks as desired, giving an improved picture of one's surroundings and the availability of linking paths. This area is exceptionally fortunate in that one single sheet give comprehensive coverage of the walks:

Outdoor Leisure Sheet 21 - South Pennines

Also extremely useful for general planning purposes are the Landranger sheets, at 1:50,000. The following cover the area:

103 - Blackburn & Burnley; 104 - Leeds, Bradford & Harrogate
109 - Manchester; 110 - Sheffield & Huddersfield

WALKING COUNTRY - CALDERDALE

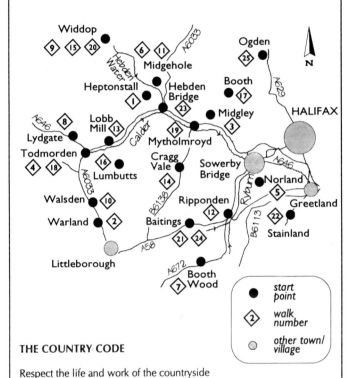

THE COUNTRY CODE

Respect the life and work of the countryside
Protect wildlife, plants and trees
Keep to public paths across farmland
Safeguard water supplies
Go carefully on country roads
Keep dogs under control
Guard against all risks of fire
Fasten all gates
Leave no litter - take it with you
Make no unnecessary noise
Leave livestock, crops and machinery alone
Use gates and stiles to cross fences, hedges and walls

ABOVE HEBDEN & COLDEN WATERS

START *Heptonstall*   *Grid ref. SD 987280*

DISTANCE *5½ miles*

ORDNANCE SURVEY MAPS
1:50,000
Landranger 103 - Blackburn & Burnley
1:25,000
Outdoor Leisure 21 - South Pennines

ACCESS *Start from the village centre. There is a car park along a side street. Heptonstall is served by bus from Hebden Bridge. An alternative start is the National Trust car park at Clough Hole on the Heptonstall-Widdop road.*

A splendid amble above two deep wooded valleys, and free of any noticeable gradients. A wedge of heather moorland divides the two.

S Heptonstall is a fascinating village that well merits an hour's leisurely exploration. Steeped in history, it was of greater importance than Hebden Bridge until the arrival of the Industrial Revolution. Happily its exposed position 850 feet up and defended on three sides by precipitous slopes has created a time warp in which its weather-beaten stone cottages revel. Focal point is the churchyard which separates the imposing parish church of 1854 from the shell of the old church of St. Thomas a'Becket, partly dating from the 13th century. 'King' David Hartley, infamous coiner is buried here - see WALK 14. Alongside is the former grammar school of 1772, now operating as a museum. Seek out also the octagonal Wesleyan chapel (1764), the old dungeon (1824) and the 16th century Cloth Hall. There are two pubs, the *Cross Inn* and the *White Lion*.

From the car park re-enter the main street and turn uphill. **Beyond the two pubs take the first turn right along Townfield Lane (opposite Weavers Square), continuing past the last of the houses as a walled green lane.** Over to the right are the deep woodlands of Hardcastle Crags, with Crimsworth Dean striking away directly ahead. **When the track emerges into a field, advance to the next wall corner ahead, then bear left across a couple of fields to join a road. Go left a short distance to a stile in the opposite wall, and go on towards a stile overlooking the valley of Hebden Water. Don't use it, but turn left along the field-side to commence a generally level course above the wooded slopes.**

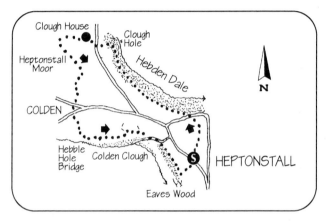

At a natural viewing platform just beyond a former quarry turn up an enclosed path, leaving it immediately by a stile on the right. Across a field bottom the original route resumes along the wood-top, though the path soon begins a steady descent through the trees. Continuing at mid-height a wide track is joined at a hairpin bend, and is followed with ease uphill. Just glimpsed down below is Gibson Mill, an early cotton mill: WALK 6 passes it in the valley of Hebden Water. Clough Hole waterfalls cannot be seen without a short scramble down the bank just before leaving the woods. A splendid series of cataracts continue down to the bottom. **The path leaves the trees and rises up to the road at Clough Hole.** Off route two minutes along to the left is Greenwood Lee, a superb example of a yeoman clothier's house. It dates from 1712 and features a splendid great barn of similar age alongside.

Waterfall, Clough Hole

Turn right past the car park then at once head up the drive to Clough House. The original path runs along the front of the house, but a new diversion might send it along the field top below the house to a path junction around the back. Take the main path rising directly away, in reedy, hollowed fashion up the pasture. Crumbling walls return as derelict Clough Head appears above, and two stiles in quick succession lead to it. Go left past the ruin to a gap in the crumbling wall corner and follow a path away with a wall on the right. This crosses to the wall ahead, where a stile admits onto Heptonstall Moor. Just in front is a cairn marking our arrival on the route of the Pennine Way.

While the main path strikes left across the moor, a drier alternative accompanies the wall left, then climbs the moor-side on a narrower path to regain the Pennine Way on the brow by the house at Mount Pleasant. At 1200ft, this is the highest point of the walk. The path goes on over the brow, being ushered left as walls close in by a lone house. Leave the moor at a gate in the left corner. Ahead are sudden views south over Jack Bridge and Colden to ever prominent Stoodley Pike.

A largely enclosed path now drops down onto a narrow road. Farm shop refreshments are often available just along to the right. A few yards to the right the path continues down a field-side to a wider road at Colden. Go straight across, past a tiny housing estate and down to Goose Hey Farm. Pass left of it, through a small gate and across to a stile just beyond. Now strike diagonally across a pasture on a part-flagged path to a stile.

A walled path descends to Colden Water, with a fork just above the beck. Well worth a brief detour just down to the right is Hebble Hole Bridge, a characterful, ancient footbridge consisting of two great stone slabs in a charming location. Here we pick up a former panniermans' way leading to Heptonstall, and the Pennine and Calderdale Ways also have one of their two meetings here. The Pennine Way is now left in favour of a better flagged path along to the left, running between the fields and the drop to the beck. On entering Foster Wood a stile is met at a kink in the accompanying wall, and here the stone causeway vacates the environs of the beck to cross several fields before losing its solid surface. A good path becomes enclosed before merging with a similar way to rise to a T-junction.

Take the track right, passing a barn to a stile where a further paved section leads to yet another enclosed path. Turn down it to join a narrow access road and head up this until a path strikes off to the right. Initially a clamber through the bouldery wood top, a grand level walk ensues high above Colden Water, soon opening out above Eaves Wood. Don't be tempted by lesser paths slanting down into the wood: it's grand, but you'll have a right pull to get back up to Heptonstall!

This final section reveals dramatic views from gritstone outcrops down the steeper heather and bilberry clad slopes into Colden Clough. Particularly grand is Stoodley Pike, seen from valley floor to the towering monument. A substantial section of slope beneath us was devastated by fire in the drought summer of 1995. The path remains with the left-hand wall until an enclosed path strikes reluctantly off to the left. The tower of Heptonstall church beckons less since hackneyed by modern housing, visible, not surprisingly, from much of upper Calderdale. To finish simply keep straight on to emerge beneath the church. Past here there are a couple of minor branches that will lead back onto the main street.

The Calder Valley from Eaves Wood, Heptonstall, looking to Stoodley Pike

2

WALSDEN MOOR

START Warland   Grid ref. SD 944200

DISTANCE 6½ miles

ORDNANCE SURVEY MAPS
1:50,000
Landranger 103 - Blackburn & Burnley
1:25,000
Outdoor Leisure 21 - South Pennines

ACCESS Start from the Bird i'th' Hand. Roadside parking beside the pub's patrons' car park. Served by Todmorden-Rochdale buses.

Sustained interest from towpath to moor top. Easy to follow paths include the historic packhorse route known as Salter Rake Gate.

Ⓢ From the pub cross the road and take the lane (Warland Gate End) to cross the Rochdale Canal. A modern boundary stone by the swing bridge marks the divide between Yorkshire and Lancashire. **Keep on the lane between two houses as it starts a long climb to the moor.** At a sharp bend it becomes surfaced: whitewashed cottages on the left feature a 1655 datestone. **The drive makes a prolonged climb to a junction, swinging right to Calf Lee House. Follow the track up past the stables to a derelict farm just above, passing behind it to a tiny gate. Slant up onto a clearer track to a stile by a gate above, to then rise in harmony with the adjacent beck past some boulders.**

The grassy retaining wall of Warland Reservoir is quickly revealed. On nearing it, take either the steeper left-hand path to the top, or follow the wide track right to the southern end of the reservoir. The moorland skyline behind features Little Holder Stones and the Wool Pack Stones. **Leave the reservoir road and strike off on a path along the embankment of neighbouring Light Hazzles Reservoir.** Where these two reservoirs meet we spend a few hundred yards in Greater Manchester, whose vast urban landscape can be seen sandwiched between much closer rolling moorland to west and south.

Warland, Light Hazzles, White Holme and Blackstone Edge reservoirs were built to supply water to the Rochdale Canal. Completed in 1804, it ran 33 miles between Manchester and the Calder & Hebble Navigation at Sowerby Bridge. The demise of the canals began in 1841 when the Lancashire & Yorkshire Railway was completed. By 1922 commercial traffic had virtually ceased, and the following year the reservoirs were sold to local authorities. **At the far end of the reservoir the path swings left, still on the distinct embankment of a defunct catchwater. Nearing the shore of Warland Reservoir again we pass below the boulders of Stony Edge.** Here we find heather and gritstone in true harmony, and the vast array of stones tempt a halt for a scramble or at least a linger. **The reservoir road is regained at the reservoir's northernmost point.**

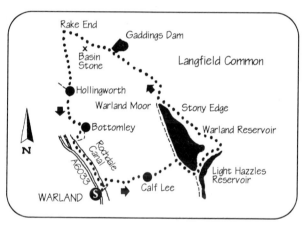

Cross the concrete drain and follow it to the right as far as a sharp bend. Stoodley Pike appears almost at once, some way along the moorland edge of Langfield Common. Down to the left is Gaddings Dam, backed by the Coal Clough windfarm spread right across the noble breast of Pendle Hill. **Now strike off left across the moor on a path in the direction of Gaddings Dam. A little moist in parts, it skirts a miniature boulderfield and improves in quality to traverse the left-hand embankment.** Note the old embankment of its former twin over to the right. **Below a flight of steps the path continues down the moor, past the Basin Stone and trending right (where faint, it aims across the moor in the direction of the windfarm rather than descending to the left).** Several standing stones shadow the path hereabouts.

A little over half a mile beyond Gaddings Dam a crossroads with a part paved way is reached, marked by a cairn, just short of Rake End. From here towards Bottomley we follow the well-preserved causeway of Salter Rake Gate, part of a packhorse route used for bringing salt across the Pennines from Cheshire. The rake has a bird's-eye view of Walsden and across the valley to Ramsden Clough. **Turn left on the path sloping down across the moor, acquiring a continuous causeyed surface. It takes in an easily by-passed marshy section before entering walled confines at North Hollingworth. Advance along the first drive a short way, and at the junction, with a white-walled old house in front, go left along the drive to South Hollingworth.**

From a gate beneath the house ignore the wide track up the field and instead trace the causeway along the field bottom. Here enjoy a fine viewpoint above Dean Royd, with the canal leading the eye through the Walsden Gorge, and the buttress of Reddyshore Scout opposite. **At the next gate it descends to the back of Dean Royd, then rises left again to a footbridge over a tiny beck. Across, enter the hamlet of Bottomley.** This was the site of an early Friends' Meeting House. **Turn right a few yards then leave the access road by a gate on the right. A superb cobbled way descends to the Rochdale Canal at Bottomley Lock.** Hidden in a field here is the northern entrance to the Summit railway tunnel, scene of a dramatic train fire in 1984. **Go left along the towpath to return to Warland, passing Warland Lower Lock and a reedy pond before finishing along Warland Gate End.**

Winter on Walsden Moor

Above: Stony Edge from the reservoir drain

Right: the Basin Stone

3

MIDGLEY MOOR

START *Midgley*   *Grid ref. SE 030263*

DISTANCE *6¼ miles*

ORDNANCE SURVEY MAPS
1:50,000
Landranger 104 - Leeds, Bradford & Harrogate
1:25,000
Outdoor Leisure 21 - South Pennines

ACCESS *Start from the village centre. Parking is limited to a few considerate roadside spaces. Midgley is served by bus from Halifax via Sowerby Bridge and Luddenden Foot, and is only one mile away from Mytholmroyd railway station. An alternative start is Jerusalem Farm, Luddenden (just off route - see map).*

A breezy encounter with heather moorland and a simple stroll down the side of a well wooded valley.

S Midgley clings tightly to the hillside beneath the moor, its houses strung out along its main street, Towngate. At the eastern end is the quite recently closed pub, the *Sportsman*, while further downhill towards Luddenden Foot are the Post office/store and school. Moving west from the former pub, we pass the following: Lydgate Well, a spring with two troughs; the Midgley Co-operative Industrial Society of 1865, currently a bookbinders; New House Farm dated 1811; Great House, a 17th century farm with mullioned windows; a house opposite the bus terminus with a curious tablet above the door; and the village stocks in a lovely corner with Town Syke Well alongside.

Follow the road through the village towards the western end, noting the above features now or at the end, depending on where you began. Just after the little row labelled Dove's Rest (1888) turn right up Frank Lane, reached before Chapel Lane at the end. Just to the right is a white-walled former weaver's cottage with a 1601 datestone. **Continue up the lane.** On the left is the enormous former Providence Methodist Chapel of 1883. **Swing left in front of a lone house higher up to a T-junction with Chapel Lane just above the old chapel.**

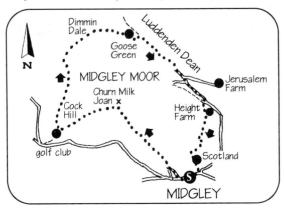

Turn right, briefly, then in front of a house at the top, bear left on the grassy continuation which rises through colourful vegetation. Early in the walk we have bird's-eye views of the Mytholmroyd area: from the outset, the monument on Stoodley Pike has been prominent. To its left the deep trough of Cragg Vale strikes into the heart of the moors southwards. **Beyond a gate continue up to the left on the top side of a sunken way, and from a stile in an intervening fence rise over the open moor to meet the level course of the Calderdale Way.** Midgley Moor is an extensive heather tract enjoyed by grouse until August.

Go left with this path which soon begins a steady rise above old quarries to a wall-corner, with an unmissable standing stone a few yards higher. This sturdy six-footer goes by the name of Churn Milk Joan, and was possibly a medieval cross (illustrated on page one). **Turn left on the clear path above the wall until the wall turns sharp left. From the wall corner the path strikes left across the moor, incorporating a newly flagged section to reach a stile in a fence ahead. A broader track drops down a little towards a building below.** This is Mount Skip golf clubhouse, at this point we earn a sudden view over Hebden Bridge and Heptonstall. **Remaining on the moor the wide path contours round above the golf course and below old quarries in a great loop under Cock Hill, then heads north with the intake wall and fence.**

A good path now takes us along the moor bottom, with the minor Sheep Stones Edge above. The path is only vacated when it turns sharp left with the wall. Here a cairn signifies the presence of a junction, from where another path heads sharp right up the moor. After a short climb it levels out to run alongside a row of crumbling stone shooting butts crossing the ridge in the depression known as **Dimmin Dale.** On the brow Luddenden Dean appears with the Ovenden Moor windfarm on its skyline. **The path by the butts soon drops down towards the Luddenden Dean side of the moor, bearing right to a crumbling wall corner at the well defined moor edge.** There are superb views into Luddenden Dean from the moor edge here, with the reservoirs visible up the valley.

While a thin path runs along the edge, our bridleway begins to descend, doubling back briefly to the wall. Note the ruin of Castle Carr's old gatehouse in the trees up dale. Castle Carr was a massive Victorian castle built amidst delightful ornamental gardens. It was later abandoned, fell into neglect and was finally dismantled in 1961. Down below, meanwhile, is the lower lodge. **A well graded slope works down to the right, and this sound path leaves the moor at a gate just above Goose Green. A splendid green pathway winds down between walls to a narrow access lane. Turn right along this firm track for a short mile, becoming fully surfaced just short of a junction with a hairpin bend.** Jerusalem Farm is just down to the left.

Head up the road to the right, soon levelling out to run on narrowly above a chain of rather nice dwellings in old farms before rising again to a junction with High House Lane. Turn right a few yards to the road end and then left up a farm drive. On approaching Height Farm take a stile on the right to regain the heather of **Midgley Moor**, again on the Calderdale Way.

An excellent path runs above the wall, all too soon reaching a stile when a fence takes over. Here drop down to the head of a drive. At the second house, turn sharp right along the Moorside farm drive. When it rises to the farm in the second field, keep straight on the field bottom to the far wall corner. Ignore the obvious stile ahead, but opt for a very slim gap-stile on the left. An old path descends the fieldside to pass right of a row of cottages at Scotland. Continue down a surprising stepped path through the last field to **Tray Royd.** This proves to be a very characterful residence with mullioned windows and a 1700 datestone. **The flagged Tray Royd Lane descends to the road in the village.**

FREEHOLDS TOP

START *Todmorden*   *Grid ref. SD 936241*

DISTANCE *8 miles (or 6½ miles)*

ORDNANCE SURVEY MAPS
1:50,000
Landranger 103 - Blackburn & Burnley
1:25,000
Outdoor Leisure 21 - South Pennines

ACCESS *Start from the town centre. Ample car parks. Served by bus and train from Hebden Bridge/Halifax and Rochdale, and by bus from Burnley. An alternative start at Gauxholme (junction of A681 Bacup road, a short mile south of town centre) saves 1½ miles. This omits the canal section, but parking is limited: served by bus from Todmorden.*

A reasonably strenuous ramble in typical Upper Calder country, with broad uplands atop steep gradients from the industrial valley.

❺ Todmorden is described on page 66. **From the roundabout head south on the Rochdale road.** On the right, just yards up Rise Lane is Todmorden Old Hall, built in 1603 by the Ratcliffe family, who long preceded the Fieldens in Todmorden circles. This 17th century house has a magnificently intricate frontage of gables and mullioned and transomed windows, and is currently a restaurant. **At the canal bridge turn right along the towpath.** Before leaving note the old horse tunnel under the main road. For more on the Rochdale Canal see page 41.

The towpath runs on. Across the canal the monstrously high railway embankment wall is a monument in its own right. **Several locks are encountered and we pass under the railway before reaching the Bacup road at Gauxholme. Pass under and turn up onto the road.** A long, low railway viaduct straddles the junction, with the *Masons Arms* sheltering beneath. **Cross the canal bridge and head away.**

Turn left off the road almost at once along short-lived Naze Road. Take a gate on the left at the end, and a broad green track heads away. Doubling back almost at once, a steep climb of the Naze ensues. This next mile traces an old packhorse route from Todmorden towards Rochdale. The climb up the Naze is a cleverly engineered zigzag. The map-like view of the cramped industrial valley floor with its railway, road, canal and mills, is in stark contrast with the hillside's crumbling walls, reedy pastures and derelict farmsteads.

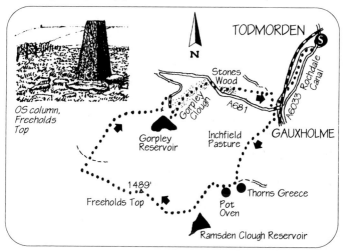

As the gradient eases the climb continues between old walls to a brief enclosed section onto the open moor. **Go forward to join a wide track, but when it bears left at a wall corner take the lesser fork straight ahead, to trace a stone causey across the moorland of Inchfield Pasture. At a beck crossing the path deteriorates, but keep straight on, going left of a pond to join the broad, unsurfaced Foul Clough Road by Thorns Greece Farm. Turn right along it, sweeping round above the intake wall to a stile and gate above the last house.**

Down to the left is Ramsden Clough Reservoir, completed in 1888 to supply Todmorden. From above it blends in well, its waters lapping the steep slope of Ramsden Hill. A North West Water notice on the gate might arouse curiosity, being as we are in Yorkshire. The answer goes back a century, for within a decade of completion, Rochdale bought Todmorden's waterworks, and Ramsden Clough remained in their hands to the present day, in the guise of their successors.

The improved track continues between crumbling walls to a fork: take the right one to maintain the climb, by and then over a lively beck. Pass near the ruin of Coolam to a gate in a fence giving access to the moor beyond. Take the firmer track rising right with the fence, then running on to the grassed over spoil and ruinous walls of an old mine. Here take a narrow trod rising behind: during its short, steep climb on easy grass it pulls half-right to impressively gain the Ordnance Survey column (S4444) on Freeholds Top.

Gorpley Reservoir in winter

At 1489ft, Freeholds Top is one of the highest points in Calderdale, and is an extensive viewpoint. Its panorama is very much an upland one: higher landmarks occupy the Pennine watershed to north and south in the shape of Black Hameldon and Blackstone Edge respectively, while to the east is Stoodley Pike, and westwards the industry-ravaged moors of Rossendale. A welcome intrusion through the Cliviger Gorge is the unmistakable outline of Pendle Hill.

From the top cross the adjacent stile and go left with the fence to a junction, there turning right with the fence and old wall along the broad ridge top. The county boundary with Lancashire occupies this section. As the fence parts company keep straight on, a rather exceptional wall is soon to take its place. When this wall returns to normal a boggy pool will be seen over the replacement wall. Only 40 yards beyond it a stile is reached: do not use it, but instead depart the ridge by descending directly away across surprisingly dry grass to join an old mine road at some former workings.

Cross straight over and down to the head of a deep clough (Range Hoyle), trending left to a collapsed wall rising away. Follow this round to the left and then away as it skirts the pronounced drop to Gorpley Reservoir. A fence soon takes over and the pathless march

continues until a farm track materialises. On nearing the reservoir note a spectacular deep cleft on its opposite bank, with a tiny finger of water reaching in: one might forget its artificial nature. Completed in 1904, Gorpley Reservoir was Todmorden's replacement for Ramsden Clough. **The pleasant track improves progress, and soon drops down to a small house. Go left along the drive and down to meet a road. Turn right to descend to the treatment plant below the dam.**

Alongside the plant take a gate on the left to descend a part-stepped path into Gorpley Clough. This is a charming wooded dell with a tinkling beck enjoying two enchanting moments, the lower cascade being especially delectable. The path through the length of the clough has enjoyed major restoration work. **This same path leads unerringly down, crossing and recrossing the beck to emerge onto the Bacup road. Turn right a short way then escape at a gap on the left beyond a house, on a path rising through Stones Wood.**

At a kissing-gate it leaves the wood to cross two fields to a junction of green ways: rise left between walls, and at the top turn right to cross a field bottom. From a stile at the end go on past a stable block. The way runs on past the buildings, turning right at the end, down the house side and left a few yards to a miniscule green way. This meets a steep track dramatically perched above the valley. The first heather of the walk is in evidence at this late stage, but it is the amazing bird's-eye view that will hold the attention. If a train should rumble along, one could be forgiven for thinking this was toytown. **Turn down the path to return to Gauxholme and retrace steps along the towpath.**

*Waterfall,
Gorpley Clough*

NORLAND MOOR

START Norland   Grid ref. SE 065224

DISTANCE 4¼ miles

ORDNANCE SURVEY MAPS
1:50,000
Landranger 104 - Leeds, Bradford & Harrogate
1:25,000
Outdoor Leisure 21 - South Pennines

ACCESS Start from the crossroads of Shaw Lane, Clough Road and Berry Moor Road by the war memorial. A secretive car park is found just off Shaw Lane, by a play area on a corner of the moor. Served by bus from Halifax via Greetland, and infrequently from Sowerby Bridge.

An easy stroll round a popular local haunt. Colourful surroundings and wide views.

S Scattered Norland 'Town' is an isolated hilltop settlement boasting some splendid clothiers' houses of centuries past. Some of these will be revealed towards the end of the walk. Of greater relevance at the outset is Norland Moor, an island-like heather tract perched high above Sowerby Bridge and the Ryburn Valley. Publicly owned for over half a century, it bears the much healed scars of extensive small-scale quarrying, notably along the western escarpment. Immediately north of the moor the sprawl of Halifax dominates.

From the car park take the broad path rising diagonally away to the heathery old quarries on the brow. The path bears along to the right, by quarry sites and along a gentle but obvious edge. Numerous sites are passed as the path runs on, absorbing a broad, sandy path alongside a covered reservoir. A little further, the more extensive quarries of Turgate Delph are passed. Just below is the *Moorcock Inn*: a quarrymans' track runs down to it for emergency refreshment!

Remaining on the edge above the quarries, the Ordnance Survey column (S4334) at 933ft offers a detour just yards to the left. Just ahead, meanwhile, is Ladstone Rock. This natural gritstone outcrop is a distinctive landmark to which is affixed a 'psalm plaque'. Extensive views westwards over the Ryburn Valley feature Crow Hill, Great Manshead Hill, Rishworth Moor, Blackstone Edge, and the moors south of the M62. Ripponden itself appears on resuming the walk.

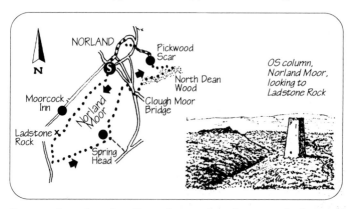

OS column,
Norland Moor,
looking to
Ladstone Rock

Resume along the edge, the path soon dropping towards the road. Without setting foot on it however, bear left across the moor, picking up a thin path running through a grassy depression. In the centre is a crossroads: bear left, rising on a better path to an old wall corner. From the crossroads of paths go straight ahead on the wallside track. It is followed its entire length, becoming enclosed on leaving the moor by some old quarries, but remaining moor-like to a bend where a farm drive comes in. **Here turn left through a gapstile, following the left-hand wall to a stile at the end.** The island farm of Spring Head is on the left. **Resume on the other side of the wall to a stile back onto the moor.**

Advance a few yards to join a broad path. Turn right along it, remaining close to the moor edge as it runs on to absorb the Calderdale Way at a cairn. Ahead the Wainhouse Tower gains in prominence, completely dwarfing the many mill chimneys and church spires. This famous landmark was built in the 1870s to serve a dyeworks, and is usually open for ascents on public holidays. **Keep on to the wall corner near the edge of the moor. At this crossroads, under a pylon, turn right to a road junction at Clough Moor Bridge.**

Immediately upstream note the old slabby bridge, and across, the old boundary stone set into the other side of the bridge ('Division of Norland and Elland'). **Cross the bridge, advance a few yards and take a wall-stile on the left to immediately regain moorland. A thin path runs down towards the stream then turns downstream with it.** This well made path has seen much work in recent years. It traces the beck down onto the quickly forming Maple Dean Clough, a riot of colourful vegetation on the western edge of North Dean Wood. **After crossing and re-crossing, briefly, the bottom of the wood proper is reached and the path runs along through the trees to the right. When the accompanying fence turns away, the path slants down to the left before running on a more level shelf to a fork.**

The right branch slants uphill while ours bears correspondingly down, slanting through stately beeches to approach the rear of an isolated house. Just short of it, turn down to the left on a thinner path to a gap in an old wall corner at the foot of the wood. A flagged path is followed left along the base of more woodland. The flags remain largely evident as the path runs on to a footbridge over the clough. A narrow, enclosed setted path then rises away, broadening into a track to reach the road end at the hamlet of Pickwood Scar.

Head out on the road, curving around above open country. In the near distance view note the grand 17th century house of Upper Wat Ing Farm, while down in the valley is a large railway viaduct backed by the extensive Long Wood. **At a junction at a house, take a flight of steps on the left up to a stile. An old flagged way climbs the field to another stile, then slants across to a gate and stile in the corner above. A green lane runs the few yards right onto a road.** Outstanding just down to the right is the Lower Old Hall, with a 1634 datestone and two-storey porch. **Turn left up the road.** On the right are the welcoming *Blue Ball Inn* and Fallingworth Hall, dating from 1642 with mullioned windows and another two-storey porch. **At the junction above turn right along Berry Moor Road. We pass St. Luke's church and the school to the central crossroads.**

*The Ladstone Rock,
Norland Moor*

6

HARDCASTLE CRAGS

START *Midgehole*   *Grid ref. SD 988291*

DISTANCE *5¼ miles*

ORDNANCE SURVEY MAPS
1:50,000
Landranger 103 - Blackburn & Burnley
1:25,000
Outdoor Leisure 21 - South Pennines

ACCESS *Start from the main National Trust car park for Hardcastle Crags, signposted off the Keighley road out of Hebden Bridge. Infrequent bus service from Hebden Bridge.*

The renowned woodlands of Hardcastle Crags are more than ably supported by a fine moor-edge track and a simple stroll above the colourful valley of Crimsworth Dean. Weekends usually see sizeable crowds at Hardcastle Crags.

S Hardcastle Crags is the name by which everyone in the district knows the valley of Hebden Dale, through which flows Hebden Water. The majority of this beautifully wooded, deep-cut dale is in the care of the National Trust, and attracts large crowds from far and wide. The 'Crags' themselves are actually visited on this walk. At the car park is a National Trust information caravan and often an ice cream van. Offering refreshment just across New Bridge on Hebden Water is the Midgehole Working Mens Club, affectionately known as the *Blue Pig*.

From the car park go a few yards up the drive past the solitary lodge, then fork left on a path descending to Hebden Water. Here a wide beckside path is accompanied upstream for almost a mile and a half, rarely straying far from the bank. Two sets of stepping stones give options to vary the route. Just before reaching the imposing Gibson Mill, we pass a tablet affixed to a rock in the beck, giving praise to God.

Gibson Mill was founded in 1800 as an early waterpowered cotton mill. After enlargement it ceased to operate in the 1890s, becoming a curiously-sited dance hall and even a roller-skating rink during the mid 20th century. The building still remains intact - with some related features nearby - and is an imposing sight in its wooded environs. A row of workers cottages are tagged on. Have a look round the back to see the surviving millpond and cut. **At Gibson Mill the drive is rejoined to climb above the beck, passing a wooden shelter and levelling out alongside the steep rise of Hardcastle Crags.** These invite a brief scramble just up to the left. This group of modest outcrops occupy a prominent knoll, with a tiny ridge rising well above the tree tops. As a result this airy spot is a superb vantage point.

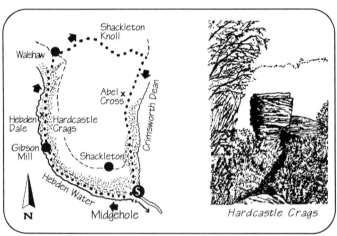

Hardcastle Crags

Continuing on from the clearing by the crags, a broad path soon forks left as the drive swings up to the right. We regain sight of the beck as the wide path gradually declines towards it. At a side beck a staggered crossroads is reached. Before the beck, the left branch doubles back to a footbridge, while our route follows the narrow path immediately after the beck. It rises through a gateway on the right and climbs steeply above the beck. At the wood-top go left a few yards to a small gate into a field, then rise to Walshaw. Approaching, the impressive front of Walshaw shooting lodge greets you. With an enviable view down-dale, the lodge dates from the 1860s: note the weather vane alongside. Walshaw is an ancient settlement, now a farming hamlet in the ownership of the Saville estate.

Just to the right of the lodge a tiny enclosure is entered by a gate and left by a stile. Head up the yard and turn sharp right on the drive for a few yards then take a gate on the left. A walled track heads away, soon becoming unenclosed and after crossing a tiny beck, rising round the top of a larger pasture. This route from Walshaw to the foot of Coppy Lane was part of a 17th century trade route, bringing lime from Lancashire to farms in the Calder Valley. **Almost at the corner a gate transfers us onto open moor, and a broad wall-side track contours round to the right beneath Shackleton Knoll.** At 1215ft the highest point of the walk is reached, and ubiquitous features of the view are Heptonstall church and the Stoodley Pike monument.

As the environs of Crimsworth Dean are entered, the moor is left at a gate from where the enclosed Coppy Lane descends past a ruin to a T-junction at Nook, another ruin. Turn right along a broader track running parallel with Crimsworth Dean Beck down to the left. Crimsworth Dean is seen in more detail on WALK 11. **This very track returns unfailingly to Midgehole, the only interruption being a diversion to inspect Abel Cross. This is found just beyond a cattle-grid after the first farm buildings at Laithe, where a stile lurks in the low wall on the right. Contour across the field to a farm drive, with Abel Cross just ahead.** It is in fact two identical shafts, thought to have been erected on a medieval pack-route. **Regain the main track to enter woodland and continue a long, gradual descent to finish.**

Abel Cross, Crimsworth Dean

```
┌─────────────────────────────────────────┐
│                  ╭───╮                   │
│                  │ 7 │                   │
│                  ╰───╯                   │
│                                          │
│       RISHWORTH MOOR                     │
│                                          │
└─────────────────────────────────────────┘
```

START *Booth Wood*   *Grid ref. SE 019161*

DISTANCE *5¼ miles*

ORDNANCE SURVEY MAPS
1:50,000
Landranger 109 - Manchester (tiny section)
*   110 - Sheffield & Huddersfield*
1:25,000
Outdoor Leisure 21 - South Pennines

ACCESS *Start from the A672 Oldham road where it gains the open moor, half a mile west of the Turnpike Inn (further parking available along the moor road) at Booth Wood Reservoir. Served by Halifax-Oldham buses.*

An invigorating ramble over archetypal Pennine moorland: very little climbing involved, though in poor conditions the upper section might prove trying. Apart from the final mile, all the walking is on the urban common of Rishworth Moor. The paths are permissive ones devised in conjunction with Yorkshire Water.

❺ Almost immediately after emerging onto Rishworth Moor the A672 passes defunct quarries on either side. Down below are the great cliffs of Derby Delph (a 'delph' being a quarry). Here stone for Green Withens Reservoir was won, and carried on a 3½ft gauge railway up Green Withens Clough to the dam. From here to just short of the reservoir our steps are along the old line, a fascinating journey! In recent years the quarry has been wardened by the RSPB, since being identified as a breeding site of the peregrine falcon: visitors are welcome in spring and early summer when the 'watch' is on. The entrance is just back down the road.

Immediately after Derby Delph a guidepost indicates a footpath branching off to the left. Though narrow, it quickly becomes clear to follow a near level course along the narrow, bracken clad strip between Booth Dean and the road above. Down below is the very upper reach of Booth Wood Reservoir. With its mighty dam almost a mile down valley, the 50 acre reservoir was completed in 1971. Lower and Upper Booth Dean Reservoirs immediately upstream are very slender and attractive neighbours, completed in 1923 to supply water to Wakefield. Immediately south of Booth Dean the M62 climbs to its summit at Windy Hill, where a mast tops the skyline. **Beyond the last reservoir the path soon rises to the road at Oxygrains Bridge.** At the confluence below, and entirely dwarfed by the modern bridge, is an outstanding example of an old packhorse bridge (see page 3).

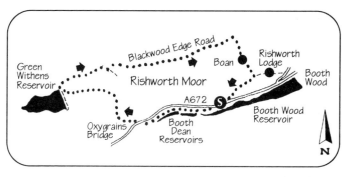

Cross the road (but not the bridge) and head up the valley of Oxygrains on a splendid green path, still the old rail line. At a knoll the valley in front proves to be merely the side valley of Wolden Edge Clough, and our main one is revealed striking up to the right. **The path runs on to the rugged environs of Castle Green Rocks.** This vicinity makes an idyllic refreshment halt: note the vertical drop from our path above the highest point. **Rising above the rocks the path swings round with the beck through Green Withens Clough to see the dam of Green Withens Reservoir high in front.**

Occasionally sketchy, the path heads for the dam, virtually to its foot before rising to the right alongside the outflow to emerge at its northern end. If in evidence the colourful sails of boats on the water present a startling contrast to this sombre upland scene, with the brooding mass of Blackstone Edge beyond the head of the reservoir. Completed in 1898 by Wakefield Corporation, the reservoir was enlarged in 1925. **Turn right along the reservoir road, which swings sharp right to follow the wide Green Withens Drain away beneath Green Withens Edge. Already, by the first bridge, the pronounced Whinny Nick can be discerned on the skyline ahead.**

Becoming a rougher track, it is left by crossing the fourth bridge since joining it. The path rises half-right through bracken onto the higher reaches of Rishworth Moor. Beyond a beck crossing it falters. Continue by rising slightly to the head of another tiny beck, then aim for the conspicuous Whinny Nick, joining an old sunken way to rise to it: just below it are some prominent spoil heaps. At 1350ft, this is the highest point of the walk. **From here the view eastwards opens up, and it is this direction we take, by keeping higher ground to the left and following a grassy strip, descending imperceptibly between peat groughs above and wetter terrain below.**

Very quickly merge with a better defined grassy path from the right, continuing on through a rash of stones from where a reedy ditch accompanies us. Soon the clearer path forks right, but our way remains with the ditch: a little further the ditch appears to fork, and a cairn on a prominent boulder (with benchmark) confirms that left is the way to go. The slopes to the left have by now diminished to the extent that there is a wide view to the north, with no uphill work needed to gain the north side of this broad tongue. At well defined Blackwood Edge this sunken way and an improving path turn right.

From Blackwood Edge enjoy extensive views north over the upper Ryburn Valley, with Ovenden Moor windfarm on the skyline beyond. Blackwood Edge Road, which we are travelling, originally serviced the moorland quarries. **The path now contours above the steeper drop to reach a tall ladder-stile in an intervening wall which should be seen well in advance.** The sunken way has remained with us, and as it goes through the gate by the stile, confirms itself as the old road.

Without crossing the stile turn right on a path over the brow of the moor, veering right to a stile in a facing wall. The lush green pastures we enter are a shock after the miles of rough moorland. **Descend a couple of fields to stiles right of the farm buildings at Boan then join its drive to go down to a sharp bend.** To visit Booth Wood dam go left. **The main route takes the kissing-gate on the right from where a green track heads away through scattered pines, then becoming enclosed by walls to finish, appropriately, back on the moor, joining the road at the old quarries where the walk began.**

(8)

BRIDE STONES

START Lydgate   Grid ref. SD 923255

DISTANCE 6¼ miles

ORDNANCE SURVEY MAPS
1:50,000
Landranger 103 - Blackburn & Burnley
1:25,000
Outdoor Leisure 21 - South Pennines

ACCESS Lydgate is 1¼ miles north-west of Todmorden on the Burnley road (A646). There is street parking in the vicinity of the Post office, and a large car park by the enormous Mons Mill nearer Todmorden centre. Served by Todmorden-Burnley buses.

A fascinating ramble around the rock formations on the hillside above Todmorden, also featuring some outstanding causeyed packways.

❺ Leave the main road by Church Road next to the Post office, and at the end bear right on a private looking drive. An enclosed footpath passes to the right of the last house and runs on darkly to emerge at an immense railway arch. Pass underneath it on a drive which rises past Stannally, steeply through trees and then a gate onto the open country of Stannally Stones. Prominent over to the left are Orchan Rocks: when you reach these, the walk is almost over!

Here the track swings right, but our route takes the path climbing straight up through heather and bracken to join a walled green lane by a stile at the top corner. This splendid track is the old packhorse route of Stony Lane, with which we are to become well acquainted. The views are very typical Calderdale: windfarm, populated valley floor, moors, farms, rocks, and Cliviger and Walsden gorges.

Turn right along the splendid track, soon emerging to cross a pasture on flags to reach Whirlaw Common. Take the main path bearing right, a superb flagged way curving beneath Whirlaw Stones. Whirlaw forms a well defined edge high above our causeway, gritstone rocks interlaced with patches of heather. **The way becomes enclosed at the end. A couple of minutes further, above East Whirlaw Farm, take a gateway on the left and follow a rough wall-side track climbing up. A little left of the wall a better track affords easier progress and rises to a gap-stile at the top right-hand corner.**

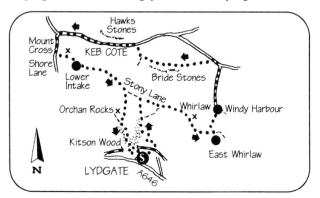

The terminus of **Windy Harbour Lane** is joined at a modest cross-roads, and after an initial pull past a mast it runs on to meet Eastwood Road. Ahead is a vast sweep of moorland. **Go left only as far as the end of the left-hand wall, where a stile sends a green path across Bride Stones Moor to the prominent outcrops of the same name.** The Great Bride Stones are the most extensive group of rocks met, and the true Bride Stone is a particularly remarkable detached rock resembling its North York Moors' namesakes. Some climbing is practised around here. The Ordnance Survey column (S4501) at 1435ft marks the highest point of the walk. **On traversing the stones the path fades, but simply continue on to a further cluster of outcrops in line with the Coal Clough windfarm immediately above Bride Stones Farm.**

From there bear right above a broken fence on the line of the stones, (note a memorial painted onto a rock face) a track soon coming in on the right to lead to a stile onto a farm road beyond the last rocks. **Turn right onto Keb Road.** The *Sportsmans Arms* is just two minutes along to the right, if needed. **The route goes left along the road for an easy mile through the scattered settlement of Keb Cote.**

Known as the Long Causeway, this ancient route between Burnley and Halifax affords extensive views to high moorland skylines. High above us are the Hawks Stones, a line of outcrops resembling bears on hind legs, while passed on the left are some interesting old commercial vehicles awaiting restoration. Note also a roadside stone inscribed 'Hawk Stones 1902'. **At the first junction (with the familiar whaleback of Pendle in view far ahead) turn left down Shore Lane just as far as a walled track opposite a farm on the right.**

This spot is a junction of packhorse routes, as Shore Lane meets the rough Stony Lane. **First encountered during the approach to Whirlaw, Stony Lane's near level course is now followed in that direction. Almost immediately a glance over the upper wall will reveal Mount Cross.** Stood forlornly amidst munching sheep, Mount Cross is thought to date back to monastic times, as a waymarker on a route serving Whalley Abbey in the Ribble Valley. **Just beyond, at Lower Intake, the way has a brief narrow section as it passes left of the farm, then resumes as a broad track. After about a mile, at the brow beyond a bridge over Redmires Water, take a stile on the right and follow a wall-side track down past the flat-topped Orchan Rocks.**

At the very bottom corner the track goes through a gate: from it drop down to the left to meet another track in another corner. Here it become enclosed, at once absorbing a farm drive which leads all the way down, largely through the trees of Kitson Wood, to the valley bottom. During this section the railway passes through a tunnel directly beneath us. **As civilisation is embraced turn left after the first house to a steep drop onto the side street on which the walk commenced.**

Bride Stones

Mount Cross

Whirlaw

9

BLAKE DEAN & WALSHAW DEAN

START *Widdop*   *Grid ref. SD 946323*

DISTANCE *6½ miles*

ORDNANCE SURVEY MAPS
1:50,000
Landranger 103 - Blackburn & Burnley
1:25,000
Outdoor Leisure 21 - South Pennines

ACCESS *Start from the roadside parking area near Clough Foot, half a mile west of the Pack Horse inn on the Colne-Heptonstall road.*

Good paths traverse the open country around the head of Hardcastle Crags. From rock strewn and part wooded valley the route takes to contrastingly bare heather moorland.

• *IMPORTANT* The path from Walshaw to Walshaw Dean is a permissive path on Savile Estate land, and may be closed on certain days in the grouse shooting season and at times of high fire risk. On such occasions a red flag is flown at the start of the path. An alternative, avoiding retracing steps, is mentioned at the relevant point.

⑤ **From the lay-by follow the road south-east towards the *Pack Horse*, but beyond a lone house take a gate on the right giving access to a short-lived green way. At the end go left with a crumbling wall along the edge of the deep little clough. The path soon starts to descend to the right to the narrow valley bottom of Graining Water.** Though our main route doesn't use it, a flagged path down to the charming watersmeet is worth an early detour, though it is also well seen from above. **Instead, keep straight on by the wall. A thinner path skirts the pronounced drop, becoming clearer when the old wall**

parts company and the gritstone outcrops of Ridge Scout appear. In the vicinity of the boulders opt for the second right-hand fork, the path improving to run beneath the largest outcrops to a kissing-gate.

The road is rejoined at a hairpin bend. The house in front is on the site of Blake Dean Baptist Chapel (1802): the burial ground survives alongside. **Turn down to the bridge and take a drive on the left, leaving it at the first opportunity to drop down to a wooden footbridge over Alcomden Water in Blake Dean.** Blake Dean is the archetypal beauty spot, a colourful watersmeet with grassy banks and green islands beneath steep bracken and gritstone studded slopes.

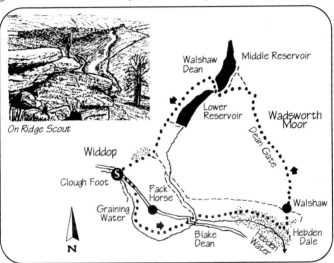

On Ridge Scout

Take the path climbing away, and when a broad green path comes on from a former railway cutting, turn right along it. Down below, five footings can clearly be seen: these supported a 700ft long trestle viaduct which carried a steam powered railway 100ft above the beck. The course of the line is also clearly discernible. It was constructed in 1901 to transport materials to the reservoir site in Walshaw Dean, of which more later. **From the stile at the end a narrower path runs through bracken, then through and above woodland to Over Wood, an extremely isolated house. Here a cart track takes over to head into deeper woods at the head of Hebden Dale.** Better known as Hardcastle Crags, the valley downstream from here is explored in WALK 6.

After about ten minutes, as we reach the floor of the valley, an inflowing beck is reached just short of a fork. Ignoring both options, instead take a narrow path up the near side of the side-stream. Passing through a gateway in an old wall, it climbs steeply to the top of the woods. At the wall go left to a small gate, and rise directly up the field to Walshaw. Approaching, the impressive front of Walshaw shooting lodge greets you. With its enviable view down-dale, the lodge dates from the 1860s: note the weather vane alongside. Walshaw is an ancient settlement, now a farming hamlet, part of the Saville estate.

A little to its right a small enclosure is entered by a gate and left by a stile. The enclosed track rising directly from the top end of the yard is our route, assuming a red flag is not flying. If it should be, then turn left on the broad bridleway track between the buildings, and it runs unerringly on to rejoin the main route near the walk's conclusion.

On heading up the track, be ready to leave it as soon as it turns sharp left to New Cote Farm, by branching off up the untidy little tract of land. Head up to a gate in the angle of a short length of fence, then rise up the fell side on a track which improves shortly after becoming enclosed. On debouching onto the moor head straight up the narrow path, which breasts a high shoulder of Wadsworth Moor. Known as Dean Gate, this path attains the summit of the walk at 1380ft. The path then drops towards the reservoirs of Walshaw Dean. At a brace of shooting boxes the shooters' track is joined and followed down to the left.

Beyond a stile the Pennine Way is joined at the end of the dam of Walshaw Dean Middle Reservoir, which is then crossed. The trio of reservoirs occupying the floor of Walshaw Dean was begun in 1900 and officially opened in 1907, but leakage problems meant the job was only fully completed in 1915. With three reservoirs under construction simultaneously, the workforce peaked at more than 500 men. Most of these were accommodated at a 'shanty town' that sprang up around the depot and offices at Dawson City, as the temporary settlement quickly became known. The site was located just north of Heptonstall overlooking Hebden Dale, where one can easily visualise a 'wild west' scene. From the middle reservoir the Pennine Way climbs over the moor to enter 'Bronteland' at the ruin of Withins.

Turning left at the end, the reservoir road is followed back to the start, avoiding all forks to the left. At a bend just before the road a stile on the left cuts out a small corner to gain the lay-by.

REDDYSHORE SCOUT

START *Walsden* Grid ref. *SD 935212*

DISTANCE *4 miles*

ORDNANCE SURVEY MAPS
1:50,000
Landranger 103 - Blackburn & Burnley
109 - Manchester
1:25,000
Outdoor Leisure 21 - South Pennines

ACCESS *Start from the south end of the village by the Waggon & Horses pub. There are various off-road parking places. Walsden is served by Todmorden-Rochdale and Todmorden local buses, and has its own railway station.*

Superb walking on green tracks through the impressive surrounds of the Walsden gorge. Quite a history trail, as well.

S Walsden is Todmorden's sizeable southerly offshoot, occupying the narrow valley floor of the little seen Walsden Water for some considerable length. Like Todmorden, it was part of Lancashire until the late 19th century, and its 'recent' industrial past focused more on cotton. Today Walsden is best known for its extensive garden centre, which draws folk from far and wide. South of the village, and for all our upland route, the railway burrows through the infamous Summit Tunnel, opened in 1840 and the scene of a dramatic train fire in 1984. Innumerable air shafts are seen on the walk.

Leave Walsden by taking the Rochdale road (A6033) and turning up an overgrown, enclosed path on the near side of the *Waggon & Horses*. At the top the surfaced Allescholes farm road is met: a

broader green way opposite cuts another corner of the road before following it up easier gradients. It soon levels completely to pass the neighbouring Allescholes farms and along to a very sudden demise at a gate onto reedy rough pasture.

A good level track heads away, quickly passing the Allescholes milestone. Impressively perched on the hilltop only a couple of yards off the path, the milestone is nevertheless easily missed as you stride on. An outstanding specimen, it bears the (very direct) distances to Todmorden, Rochdale, Burnley and Halifax. Our outward route traces this centuries old packhorse route of Reddyshore Scout Gate high above the Summit Tunnel's course. The views over the Walsden Gorge are now excellent, featuring the Rochdale Canal backed to the south-east by the Chelburn Reservoirs (built to serve it, though one is now dry) with the knobbly landmark of Blackstone Edge behind.

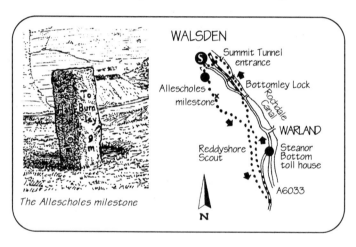

The Allescholes milestone

Immediately over the canal note the labyrinthian zigzags of old quarrymens' tracks scaling the steep slopes opposite, while the *Bird i'th' Hand* inn at Warland is seen in true bird's-eye fashion directly below. **At a gate between two pylons the way becomes enclosed, running dramatically atop the crest of Reddyshore Scout.** The steep, dark crags add a dramatic foreground to the views already described. **The track continues unfailingly, merging into a farm drive to drop eventually to the Calderbrook road.**

Turn left down the road to a boundary sign and air shaft. On the left Owler Clough offers a charming series of cascades above the road. It marks the county boundary, and set into the wall on the right is an old boundary stone (Todmorden/Littleborough). Visible at various stages on the road junction below is the Steanor Bottom Toll House. This hexagonal building stands astride a former turnpike junction, and its list of charges is admirably preserved.

At the boundary, meanwhile, take a gate on the left to follow a green path heading back towards Reddyshore Scout. This one however is to run beneath the cliffs, parallel with our outward leg. After a stile below the pylon it begins a steady descent past two more air shafts. On nearing the valley road a final air shaft is passed and a drive joined: cross straight over and down a nice cobbled snicket onto the main road.

Cross over and go left to steps joining Bottomley Road to gain access to the Rochdale Canal at Bottomley Lock. The Rochdale Canal was completed in 1804, running 33 miles between Manchester and the Calder & Hebble Navigation at Sowerby Bridge. Sadly its heyday was not a long one, and the demise began in 1841 when the Lancashire & Yorkshire Railway was completed. Thus the canals, which themselves had replaced packhorses with far greater efficiency, were quickly ousted by the vastly improved service the railways offered. By 1922 commercial traffic had virtually ceased. **Go left on the towpath, passing Sands Lock and leaving at a gap-stile fifty yards after Lightbank Lock. A path doubles back between a reedy drain and a crumbling wall. Where they end go left a little further to a white gate accessing the railway line. A tiny beck is then crossed to rise between houses onto the main road. Turn right for a quick return to the start.**

Reddyshore Scout

CRIMSWORTH DEAN & LIMER'S GATE

START *Midgehole*   *Grid ref. SD 988291*

DISTANCE *6 miles*

ORDNANCE SURVEY MAPS
1:50,000
Landranger 103 - Blackburn & Burnley
*   104 - Leeds, Bradford & Harrogate*
1:25,000
Outdoor Leisure 21 - South Pennines

ACCESS *Start from the National Trust car park at New Bridge, Midgehole. This (with overflow facilities) is the main car park for Hardcastle Crags, signposted off the Keighley road out of Hebden Bridge. Infrequent bus service from Hebden Bridge.*

After a stiff start, an easy walk ensues to combine superb woodland and beck scenery with a bracing moorland ramble.

S Hardcastle Crags is the name by which everyone in the district knows the valley of Hebden Dale, through which flows Hebden Water. The majority of this beautifully wooded, deep-cut dale is in the care of the National Trust, and attracts large crowds from far and wide. At the car park is a National Trust information caravan and often an ice cream van. Offering refreshment just across New Bridge on Hebden Water is the Midgehole Working Mens Club, affectionately known as the *Blue Pig*.

From the car park cross the bridge and take a narrow way behind the toilets. Behind a solitary house bear left and continue climbing on a stony track between crumbling walls. This superb old bridleway

winds about effortlessly to gain height through the woodland of Pecket Well Clough. As height is gained the towering Wadsworth war memorial may be seen high up to the left, and can easily be visited by branching off at some old steps from where a narrow path rises steeply left. A stile gives access to the small pasture containing the monument.

Wadsworth's war memorial is a striking edifice, a remarkable tribute to the lost sons of the parish. Perched above a colourful pocket of heather and gritstone outcrops it commands a glorious view, with Heptonstall church silhouetted and the environs of Hardcastle Crags as on a map. **The main path soon levels out to cross a beck before meeting a similar path to rise steeply onto the A6033 at Pecket Well.**

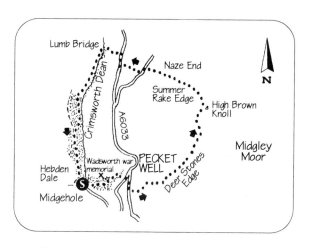

Pecket Well is an old mill community high on the moor edge: the *Robin Hood* pub is just along to the left. **Cross straight over the Hebden Bridge-Keighley road and up a short-lived path onto a wide back road, turning right along it. After a few minutes leave by the surfaced Shaw Croft Hill road up to the left. It ends at some houses but a narrow, walled path escapes to the left. It rises to an open area: either rise gradually or double back steeply up onto a broad level track. Go left a short distance then strike sharp right up another walled track. At the top it emerges onto open moorland. Keen eyes will discern the white Ordnance Survey column on High Brown Knoll, which is our objective.**

*Wadsworth War Memorial,
looking to Stoodley Pike and Heptonstall*

On the moor opt for a broad track rising half-right, but leave it within a minute by the higher of two sunken tracks rising left. After levelling out it fades before meeting a level track at a wall corner. After a few yards with the wall it turns to rise across the moor, forking into two more sunken ways which merge at the discernible **Deer Stones Edge.** Here a heather grouse moor is encountered. Ahead, Ovenden Moor windfarm appears, with the *Withens Hotel* prominent to its right. **A good path runs northwards along this largely grassy edge, fading just beyond a substantial cairn to the right. The short section to the Ordnance Survey column on High Brown Knoll is not too obvious. A thinner path bears 'inland' from the edge, around a rougher area to meet the sunken way of the Limer's Gate, and a thin path climbs above it to gain the waiting Ordnance Survey column (S4630).**

At 1453ft, High Brown Knoll is the summit of the walk. It stands a mere 20 feet below Nab Hill, 2 miles to the north-east and the highest point between the Keighley-Hebden Bridge and Keighley-Halifax roads. The extensive panorama is a distinctly moorland one. North-west of the Ordnance column is an area of cairns atop gritstone boulders. From here to Lumb Bridge we follow with minor variations the route of the Limer's Gate, a centuries-old packhorse way for transporting lime from Lancashire to the farms of the Calder Valley.

A cairned path strikes north-west above modest Summer Rake Edge, remaining clear to Naze End, with the A6033 below. Descend to a gate onto it and go left a short way. Within 100 yards a stile on the right sends a narrow path down a reedy pasture. Down below is the

deep valley of Crimsworth Dean. The path swings right at the bottom to a small gate in a wall. A narrow path (Gib Lane) descends to a quiet road. This old road to Haworth is now only a rough track where it crosses the watershed to the north. Turn right past farm buildings and from a gate on the left a deeply enclosed path (Lumb Lane), flagged in its lower stages, descends to Crimsworth Dean Beck, turning right at the bottom to Lumb Bridge and Lumb Hole waterfall. This is a stunning moment, packhorse bridge and waterfalls forming a delectable scene. Cross the bridge and head downstream, but as the main path climbs away, go left through a gateway on a narrower path.

Remaining parallel with the beck, the path contours through several bracken filled pastures, eventually encountering a stile and the humble dwelling of Outwood before reaching a gate into the National Trust woods. From it a track rises to meet the main drive which descends unfailingly to the starting point, but a more interesting variation ignores the gate in favour of a gap to its left, descending across the field to a stile into the woods.

A path runs down to the stone arched Weet Ing Bridge which is not crossed. Continue instead on the same bank, rising a little then running along towards a gate into a field. One hundred yards before it however, rise half-right (junction sketchy) to join the main drive. This is now followed down to the left all the way back to Midgehole.

The falls,
Lumb Hole

45

12

UPPER RYBURN

START *Ripponden*   *Grid ref. SE 040197*

DISTANCE *5¾ miles*

ORDNANCE SURVEY MAPS
1:50,000
Landranger 104 - Leeds, Bradford & Harrogate (tiny section)
*   110 - Sheffield & Huddersfield*
1:25,000
Outdoor Leisure 21 - South Pennines

ACCESS *Start from the parish church in the centre. There is a car park just above, over the main road. Served by bus from Halifax via Sowerby Bridge, many services continuing to Rochdale and Oldham.*

An intimate exploration of the upper reaches of the Ryburn Valley, returning along quiet roads and green lanes.

S Ripponden is a busy village, its old centre being a conservation area. The spire of St. Bartholomew's church reaches to the heavens, while alongside is a restored packhorse bridge. The white-walled and even more historic *Old Bridge Inn* is only one of a wealth of pubs. The railway arrived from Sowerby Bridge in 1881 and closed in 1958. Sections of it have now been put to use as permissive paths.

From the church do not cross either of the bridges, but pass between the houses at Bridge End and underneath the road bridge over the Ryburn. A cobbled road heads upstream, then walk through a small park onto a road. Beyond the houses and small industrial estate a riverbank track takes over, becoming a path. It rises briefly above the Ryburn at some steps to a footbridge (not used), then descends through trees to the river and on to its confluence with Booth Dean Beck. This woodland section is superb: across the river some industry remains, and several weirs testify to the traditional mill needs of times past, though today the most action they see is a heron taking flight.

Cross the inflowing beck and up Holme House Lane onto the A672, crossing that and the Ryburn simultaneously before departing left on Bar Lane, parallel with the river. It runs upstream to finally end at a mill. En route much housing is passed, then a charming millpond on the left and an almost hidden one on the right, just short of the mill. Most recently a paper mill it is currently derelict: a nice touch, until recently, was a quaint fire appliance in its own garage.

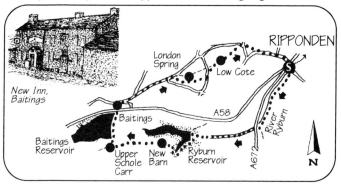

A cobbled road takes over at an underpass beneath the mill. At a hairpin bend go forward round the left of a garage, where a path is found with a millpond below and the curved concrete dam of Ryburn Reservoir spectacularly in front. At a stile take the easier route up to the right, emerging at a car park at the dam's north end before proceeding to cross it. Ryburn Reservoir was completed in 1932 for Wakefield Corporation. It is largely surrounded by woodland, and blends well in its deeper fold of the valley. This is in contrast to its more recent neighbour, the dam of which is visible up ahead. Beneath Ryburn's dam it is interesting to compare 'progress' in conserving water, the old millpond being overshadowed by the 100ft high dam.

At the far end take the track right, above the water's edge to reach a footbridge over the head of the reservoir's southern arm. A path climbs through trees into a field, then rises by a wall to become enclosed before arriving at New Barn Farm. Go right of the buildings and directly along the field behind, rising in a straight line before levelling out to run along to a stile. Over to the left is the wide span of Rishworth Moor, with the drone of the unseen M62 motorway coming from beyond it. **Continue along this pleasant crest, becoming enclosed again at the end. This is quickly left by a small gate to gain access to the Bronte-like ruin of New House just down to the right.**

From the wall corner by the ruin follow a level wall in the direction of Baitings Reservoir, soon becoming enclosed to reach a newly restored house at Upper Wormald. At the outhouse opposite leave the track by a gate to cross two fields to Upper Schole Carr Farm. Here turn right down a track to cross the dam of Baitings Reservoir. Baitings was completed as recently as 1956 on the site of a much smaller reservoir dating from the 1920s. The massive concrete dam might rapidly induce vertigo, being curiously sinuous and with unusually low walls. Hold on to your false teeth if peering over it!

Across the dam join the A58 at the well sited pub. The *New Inn* displays the interesting appendage of a large sundial. A sketchy path climbs the rough pasture behind it to a parallel road with an even more prominent white-walled inn. The *Blue Ball* is an old packhorse inn serving the route out of Lancashire over Blackstone Edge proper (see WALK 21). This was superseded by the modern turnpike road over Blackstone Edge which adopted the lower route by the pub's suitably named lower neighbour. Today the *Blue Ball* has a reputation for its choice of good ales and its extensive view over the dam to Rishworth Moor. A short verse adorns the wall above the door.

Now turn right along the quiet, level Blue Ball Road (avoiding lesser turns) for a good three-quarters of a mile. This return walk has good views over to Norland Moor and down the Ryburn to Sowerby Bridge, where it meets the Calder. At a crossroads with rough lanes just beyond a T-junction, go right on the walled track known as London Spring Road. Continue straight past London Spring Farm. Becoming less used, we even pass a pocket moor before descending onto another road, Green Lane.

Go left just a few yards before branching right down another walled track. This is Cote Road, and soon on the left we pass the splendid old house of Low Cote, with its mullioned windows and dainty gabled porch. At the far end cross straight over a road, behind a house, over a second road and along a green track. Two minutes along to the right is the *Beehive Inn*, though Ripponden itself is only ten minutes away now. Just past a house, bear right down a wall-side, quickly become tightly enclosed as a narrow green pathway descends between walls onto the narrow Royd Lane at a pleasant row of cottages. Note a 1764 datestone on the next house down.

Royd Lane leads steeply and rapidly down into the centre of Ripponden, and the car park. For the church cross the main road and down a short lane to the *Old Bridge Inn* and the packhorse bridge.

13

JUMBLE HOLE CLOUGH

START *Lobb Mill*   *Grid ref. SD 956246*

DISTANCE *5¾ miles*

ORDNANCE SURVEY MAPS
1:50,000
Landranger 103 - Blackburn & Burnley
           104 - Leeds, Bradford & Harrogate
1:25,000
Outdoor Leisure 21 - South Pennines

ACCESS *Start from the Lobb Mill car park 1½ miles east of Todmorden centre on the Hebden Bridge road. Served by Hebden Bridge-Todmorden buses. Train station in Todmorden.*

A labyrinth of hillside tracks and a towpath trod sandwich the walk's highlight, a descent of the facinating Jumble Hole Clough.

❺ **Leave the car park by the path at its eastern end, rising across the breast of a hugely colourful pocket of open country.** From the very outset we are treated to extensive views over the valley, to Stoodley Pike opposite and high moors east and west, beyond Hebden Bridge and Todmorden respectively. Below, the railway disappears beneath us into the Horsefall Tunnel. **As the green way zigzags up avoid any lesser forks and at the top the wide path becomes enclosed to approach a group of buildings at Rodwell.** Now undergoing a mini-revival, this hamlet once boasted several dozen residents in the mid 19th century. **Pass between them and on to a T-junction of walled tracks, then turn left and remain on the same track to eventually rise up to a road.**

Turn right along the road for a couple of minutes and then take a private looking drive up to the left between two houses. This is Butts Lane, which climbs steeply until turning sharply left at a lonely

49

dwelling: **here go straight up a partly-overgrown way which within a few yards meets a good path. Turn right along it, immediately through a gap-stile and across to a beck.** Less distinctly it passes above the confines of Higher Birks, a renovated farm, to meet a sunken way on the other side. Rising gently between long-collapsed walls, it doubles back a little before levelling out.

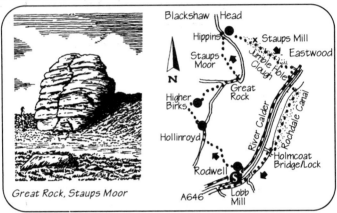

Great Rock, Staups Moor

At 1050ft this is the highest point of the walk. Note the complete disappearance of the valley floor: there is virtually no evidence that we are in industrial Calderdale, as the shelfs of lush, walled pastures that characterise this part of the dale hide the deep valley bottom. **The track runs on the field bottom as a splendid green way, becoming enclosed at the end to emerge onto a narrow road. Go left to a junction and then right to the prominent Great Rock.** Great Rock is aptly named, seeming all the more imposing for its roadside location. The inevitable carved initials and professions of undying love have been joined by the official 'vandalism' of a yellow painted Calderdale Way stencil: since the first edition of this book someone has seen fit to chisel this off! Scramble to the top and enjoy the view.

Leave the road by an enclosed track left of the rock. On debouching onto Staups Moor it turns to descend by a wall, crossing a stile into a field to drop steeply onto a road. Cross Hippins Bridge to turn immediately right on an access track. Just along it is the lovely old house at Hippins, of dark millstone grit, with mullioned windows and a 1656 datestone. **Immediately after the house take a kissing-gate in front and follow the green wall-side path away. A stile in it marks the**

point to branch off right, a path soon materialising to descend stone steps to a footbridge across the beck. Here begins the descent of Jumble Hole Clough: never too claustrophobic, it is sheer delight. Note the exceedingly delectable waterslide immediately downstream, and the line of the goit to supply Staups Mill.

Turn downstream to the ruined Staups Mill. This former cotton spinning mill occupies an evocative setting. Further down are innumerable remains of other mills and their associated workings, making it possible to visualise its industrial heyday: this little beck certainly paid its way. Past the mill the path rises, but part way up take a left fork to remain parallel with but high above the beck. After passing with care above a substantial crag the path descends to cross two field bottoms, returning into the woods to be absorbed into a farm drive. Just below an old millpond it doubles back to cross the beck, then clings to its other bank to arrive at the buildings at Jumble Hole.

Before the railway underpass turn right on a drive parallel with the line, continuing into the trees until a footbridge crosses the railway. Here we are returned to the valley floor with a jolt, to the sights and sounds of the industrial landscape. Yet through the wooded clough opposite, eyes are drawn to Stoodley Pike monument, a noble sentinel on the lofty moorland skyline. Of apparently unattainable height, it is a reminder of Calderdale's rich character. Dropping to the main road at Eastwood go right only a few yards before escaping on Burnt Acres Lane over a river bridge alongside a mill. Continue on to cross a canal bridge, then turn immediately right onto a footpath. This runs delightfully through the wood above the canal, making a fine alternative to the towpath.

The canal towpath is rejoined at the next opportunity, at Holmcoat Bridge and Lock. During the next mile we pass three locks, the odd mill, and also an interesting island-like section between canal and river. Yes, that was the Calder. For more on the canal, see page 41. Leave the towpath on reaching the lock and road bridge at Lobb Mill. Turn right to rejoin the main road by a viaduct and right again to return to the starting point.

Staups Mill, Jumble Hole Clough

STOODLEY PIKE
from Cragg Vale

START *Cragg Vale*   *Grid ref. SD 999231*

DISTANCE *7 miles*

ORDNANCE SURVEY MAPS
1:50,000
Landranger 103 - Blackburn & Burnley
*   104 - Leeds, Bradford & Harrogate*
1:25,000
Outdoor Leisure 21 - South Pennines

ACCESS *Start from the church and pub, just beneath the main road (signposted Church Bank Lane - look for the tower). Parking opposite the pub. Served by bus from Hebden Bridge via Mytholmroyd.*

Splendid beck scenery precedes a climb to breezy moorland. The walk features wonderful views and a host of fine features.

S   Cragg Vale's claim to infamy is as the home of Yorkshire Coiners. It is the most romantically recalled (though far from only) site of 18th century counterfeiting: this involved clipping gold from guineas to make additional, inferior coins. We shall later pass the house of one of the main characters. Cragg Vale's bleak moorland beginnings soon transform into a deep, richly-wooded valley before joining the Calder at Mytholmroyd. The first mile of the walk shadows Cragg Brook through fascinating terrain with numerous reminders of the mills it was made to serve. The church of St. John the Baptist in the Wilderness dates from 1840, while the *Hinchliffe Arms* sits in its dark shadow.

From the bridge by the pub take the private road on the church side of Cragg Brook, soon ending at a yard. Cross to a narrow gate between the houses from where a kerbed green path runs downstream to a bridge. Remaining on this bank, a brief choice awaits.

The main path continues on the broad track rising above the beck, past houses and on towards the road. **A nicer diversion takes a beckside path, tracing an old mill cut past a weir and on to a millpond: the path then doubles back up some steps to rejoin the track. Just before reaching the road, however, fork left at the last house, through a private looking yard and down a concrete track to another bridge.**

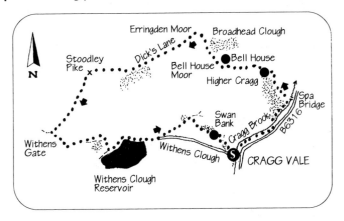

This time **cross the beck to Papermill Cottage and turn right up a broad path,** soon levelling out to run high above the steep wooded bank. When the left hand wall disappears we are immersed in the wood: **within 75 yards fork right, down towards the beck, and from a gate cross two narrow pastures to emerge onto a drive. Go down it to Spa Bridge, but then strike sharply left up a few steps, keeping with the wall to rise beneath a house (Spa Laithe) and into trees.**

On leaving the trees **follow an old way up the field. When it ends continue up beneath a wood corner, passing above a house to a stile in the top corner. Go right with a fence to a stile at the end to enter a leafy, hollowed way.** At the top **Higher Cragg Farm is reached and a track rises away.** Northwards is Mytholmroyd backed by Midgley Moor, while back over Cragg Vale Robin Hood Rocks rise above rich woodland. **Above the bend take a stile by the left-hand of two gates from where the track rises by a wall. After a fence takes over cross a stile in it and head up again, soon being deflected right by a deeply sunken way to Bell House, visible across to the right. Remain with it to a stile onto Bell House Moor, and cross a wet corner to Bell House.**

The suitably remote Bell House was the home of the coiners' leader, 'King' David Hartley. As a result of the murder of an exciseman, he was eventually hanged at York, and his grave can be seen at Heptonstall (WALK 1). **From the outside of its yard rise left on its access track to meet a stone causeway, and follow it to the right. Its surface never properly reappears after a marshy section, but the path remains clear to contour round to the unmistakable head of Broadhead Clough, locally Bell Hole.** This natural amphitheatre spectacularly scooped out of the moor is filled with a range of hardy old trees. The 'innards' are a nature reserve explored in WALK 19.

Approaching Broadhead Clough, on Bell House Moor

Leave the rim of Bell Hole by striking directly away over Erringden Moor, aiming for a highly conspicuous gate in the wall on the western skyline. Traces of a path are scant, but roughly half-way across a clear path marked by a series of upright stones is crossed at right-angles. Turn left here, rising gently up the moor. As walls close in we are drawn unfailingly to Dick's Lane, the right-hand green way. Dick's Lane is a broad green way with extensive panoramas westward to the moors enclosing Todmorden, and northward to the deep wooded confines of Jumble Hole Clough, Colden Clough and Hebden Water. Heptonstall, with its church tower is prominent on its green ridge between the latter two. Old boundary stones share Dick's Lane.

The monument on Stoodley Pike now beckons and draws us along the length of the lane, turning right at the end to a gap-stile from where the Pennine Way rises to the monument itself. En route we pass a spring: the trough's inscription *public slake trough* now appears indiscernible. On gaining the monument, Ovenden Moor windfarm is joined in the view by part of Coal Clough windfarm. For a note on Stoodley Pike please refer to page 60.

Te Deum Stone

An easy mile of the Pennine Way now ensues as the well defined escarpment to the south of the Pike is followed, eventually dropping a little through old quarries to a crossroads with a well preserved paved way. This is overseen by the Long Stoop, an old guidepost of monumental stature. Here the modern foot traveller's highway, the Pennine Way, meets a centuries old packhorse route known (like several others) as the Long Causeway. The splendidly preserved section of flags can be seen going all the way down towards Mankinholes. **Go left along the causey, the flags not surviving too far but the path remaining clear to the watershed wall at Withens Gate.**

On the other side of the stile stands the squat Te Deum Stone. Its Latin inscription is, translated, *We praise thee O Lord!*, and being on the summit of the Mankinholes-Withens track is likely to have been used for resting coffins. **Head away on the broad wall-side path beginning the descent to Withens Clough.** Ahead, Withens Clough Reservoir, completed in 1894 for Morley Corporation, is fully revealed. **When the accompanying wall ends, turn left along an inviting grassy track by a crumbling wall.**

When the track swings down to the right at an old gateway (with a gate just ahead) forsake this permissive bridleway in favour of an initially less obvious path contouring left. Becoming immediately clear, it quickly takes on a superb causeyed surface as it runs on several field-sides, with old gap-stiles in place. At the end a junction of paths is met. With the causey gone, turn down the wall-side on the right, merging into the clearer line of the bridleway to drop down to join the firm track alongside the reservoir. Turn left to the dam.

From here a surfaced road drops back down to the start, but there's a nicer finish. **Take the broad track rising left from the car park. It eases out alongside a wood, and at the end take a more inviting walled green track down to the right. This passes beneath a wood to Swan Bank Farm. One field beyond it, take a stile on the right and descend the wall-side, part causeyed. From the bottom corner go left a few yards to a gap-stile, from where a splendid raised causey runs along to the left. At a wood corner it enters the trees, running along the bottom to quickly emerge at a hairpin bend of the farm drive. Turn downhill to rejoin the Withens Clough road just short of the pub.**

15

GORPLE MOORS

START *Widdop*   *Grid ref. SD 946323*

DISTANCE *5¼ miles*

ORDNANCE SURVEY MAPS
1:50,000
Landranger 103 - Blackburn & Burnley
1:25,000
Outdoor Leisure 21 - South Pennines

ACCESS *Start from the roadside parking area half a mile west of the Pack Horse inn, where the Gorple reservoir road leaves the Heptonstall-Colne road.*

A trio of moorland waters linked by very pleasant paths and tracks. Much of this walk is on permissive paths on Yorkshire Water land.

❸ From the lay-by take the gate across the road and head away along the reservoir road with its two concrete strips. It leads first to the dam of Gorple Lower Reservoir, to then continue alongside the water and its feeder Reaps Water. Remain on it until arrival at the dam of the second sheet of water, Gorple Upper Reservoir. The two Gorple Reservoirs were completed in 1934.

Again ignore the track across the dam, and instead cross the water catchment drain on the right and take a thin path climbing directly up the slope of Shuttleworth Moor. Initially steep, it soon eases to rise through various outcrops. Some of these rock formations are impressively substantial. **The path continues up this broad tongue to join a wide track, Gorple Gate. At 1420ft, this is the highest point of** the walk. Gorple Gate is another old way over the moors to Worsthorne in Lancashire, and would have been at its busiest in packhorse days, perhaps three centuries ago.

Turn right along the track which at once begins a gentle descent.
Widdop Reservoir appears in its entirety ahead, backed by an
impressive line of crags. **After dropping steeply left to a sharp bend,
branch left on a narrower path. This now drops gradually towards
the reservoir with the remains of a wall, with some sections of old
causey featuring. Just beyond its head drop right to a footbridge. A
few yards beyond it a wide track is joined and followed right.**

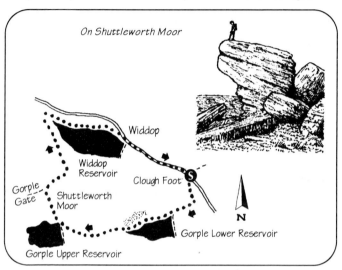

**Pass between a wall and a drain for a few yards then cross the drain
by a footbridge and head left again, infallibly between reservoir and
drain.** Widdop Reservoir was built to supply Halifax and completed
in 1878, over 50 years before the walk's two other reservoirs: it almost
equals their joint capacity. Materials reached the site by means of a
5½ mile horse-drawn tramway from further down the valley. Some
outstanding gritstone crags flank the reservoir to the north. **When the
trees disappear a better track comes in, still by the shore until
beyond an old house it recrosses the drain and heads up to the road.**

**Go right on this largely unfenced moor road, past Clough Foot to the
start.** The moorland Colne-Heptonstall road was an important trans-
Pennine packhorse route, lime and cloth being major goods. Shortly
after leaving the dam, look back over your right shoulder to see a giant
'rocking' stone perched on one of the crags on the moor edge.

16

STOODLEY PIKE
from Lumbutts

START *Lumbutts*   *Grid ref. SD 956234*

DISTANCE *7 miles*

ORDNANCE SURVEY MAPS
1:50,000
Landranger 103 - Blackburn & Burnley
1:25,000
Outdoor Leisure 21 - South Pennines

ACCESS *Start from the village centre. The dead-end road to the Top Brink inn is claimed as patrons' parking, though there are several odd corners just up the hill also. An alternative start is a roadside parking at the Shepherd's Rest, a short mile into the walk. Lumbutts is served by bus from Todmorden.*

An exhilarating high-level march around the Lumbutts and Mankinholes skyline, requiring a relatively small amount of effort.

🅢 Lumbutts is an attractive settlement nestling in a hollow below Mankinholes. It is entirely dominated by a former water wheel tower. This immense structure once contained three vertically arranged wheels, each fed from above as well as independently. It served a cotton mill that once stood here. Immediately above the tower is Lee Dam, one of three tree lined dams hovering above the hamlet. It is the scene of an annual New Year 'dip'. Also prominent is the *Top Brink*, a welcoming, sprawling hostelry.

Stoodley Pike monument is in view from the outset, but frustratingly seems to keep its distance! **From the pub descend either the enclosed path or the road by the old tower and head along the endlessly rising road.** En route note a sundial dated 1864 on the corner of a modest cottage, complete with a 'time-rhyme'. **After a long three-quarters of** a mile another hostelry, the *Shepherd's Rest*, is reached. Here take a gate on the left and follow a good track climbing steadily across the moor. Avoiding a lesser fork left fairly early, the track forks again by some old workings: the level left branch is the obvious main path.

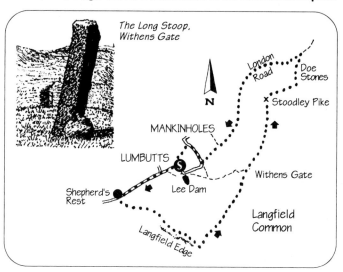

Now narrower but totally foolproof, the path rises ever gradually beneath the dark cliffs of Langfield Edge. Shapely rock formations and scars of long abandoned quarrying are in stark contrast to the flat moors immediately above. Alongside our path are the remains of a couple of former dams beneath the quarries. The conspicuous green track below us, meanwhile, is Withins New Road, a 'cotton famine' road made in 1862 to give employment at the height of a depression. Eventually our superbly engineered way gains the brooding rocks at their far end, then a path contours around the head of Black Clough and doubles back across the far side. The original path becomes sketchy as it commences a sunken descent, but a modern walker's path has taken over to avoid this loss of height. Rising gently to the right it improves a little as it runs above a well defined edge enhanced by a rash of boulders.

As the slope tails off so do the rocks, and the path heads more to the right, skirting the top of Coldwell Hill but running along towards a prominent cairn on a rock platform. From here the view opens out to the east, with Withens Clough Reservoir appearing. **Either join the unmistakable course of the Pennine Way yards to the right, or remain near the better defined 'edge' as long as possible. On the right here is a 1992 memorial seat.**

Either way the Pennine Way soon takes us north, descending slightly to a crossroads with a well preserved paved way. This is overseen by the mighty Long Stoop, an old guidepost of monumental stature. Here at Withens Gate the modern foot traveller's highway, the Pennine Way, meets a centuries old packhorse route known (like several others) as the Long Causeway. The splendidly preserved section of flags can be seen going all the way down towards Mankinholes. **Our path advances straight on, rising through an old quarry and along a broad and popular course to the Stoodley Pike monument.**

The monument on Stoodley Pike was erected in 1815 to celebrate peace after victory over Napoleon, but later collapsed and was replaced in 1856. An inscription over the door explains some of its history. It stands a mighty 120ft above the 1307ft moortop, and is the upper valley's most famous landmark. A dark, spiral staircase climbs 39 steps to a viewing balcony: the 360 degree panorama features moorland skylines in almost every direction, and a pleasing aspect is the way intervening slopes mask the industrialised valley floor.

Leave the top with the Pennine Way as it strikes eastwards. The broad path passes a spring bursting into a trough whose inscription

public slake trough now appears indiscernible. **After two neighbouring stiles the broad path drops down below the Doe Stones. On encountering a sunken quarry track in a slight depression, with the farm ahead almost hidden, turn down it to descend to a wide track, and go left to a gate. This near level track known as London Road contours beneath the Pike's steep slopes, and leads unfailingly along the foot of the common to eventually reach a corner. Keep straight on the walled track in front to drop down to the edge of Mankinholes.**

Water wheel tower, Lumbutts

60

Approaching Stoodley Pike

Mankinholes is an old handloom weaving settlement largely by-passed by the 20th century. The great water troughs are a sign of its importance in packhorse days. Most visitors today are youth hostellers breaking their Pennine Way journey in the shadow of Stoodley Pike. **Turn right through the hamlet to the last buildings, and on as far as a lone house.** This is the site of Mankinholes Methodist Church, built 1814, enlarged 1870 rebuilt 1911, closed 1979, demolished 1981. **Here turn left down the paved track known as Lumbutts Lane to return unfailingly to the start at Lumbutts.** At the very foot of the lane note an old guidepost inscribed 'Halifax' and 'Heptonstall', complete with mileages.

Mankinholes

LUDDENDEN DEAN

START Booth   Grid ref. SE 036277

DISTANCE 5 miles

ORDNANCE SURVEY MAPS
1:50,000
Landranger 104 - Leeds, Bradford & Harrogate
1:25,000
Outdoor Leisure 21 - South Pennines

ACCESS *Start from the car park at Jerusalem Farm, located half a mile west of Booth Village on Jerusalem Lane. Booth is served by bus from Halifax/Sowerby Bridge via Luddenden Foot.*

S Jerusalem Farm is operated by Calderdale Countryside Service as an education and training centre. **From the farm turn back down the road towards Booth. Beyond the trees, a gap-stile is hidden on the left. From it drop down the wall-side onto the main road through Booth.** Opposite is the Independent Sabbath School of 1850, converted into dwellings. **Cross diagonally right and go down steps and cobbles past a graveyard to a lower road at a long row of houses at Goitside. Turn right to a cobbled fork. Bear left, then ignore the next branch left, over the brook, and keep straight on the broad track.**

This runs on to two final houses, and the bridleway continues into trees. **Very soon it emerges at another row of houses, Brook Terrace. At the end keep to the right branch, which quickly narrows back to a bridleway.** All around are ruins of old mills. **The bridleway remains in the company of the brook to a fork just short of Luddenden village. Either takes you into the centre, the left one going via the church.**

Luddenden is a charming village oozing with character but free of tourists. At the centre are pub and church. The *Lord Nelson* is an attractive place sporting a 1634 datestone: Branwell Bronte drank here when employed as ticket clerk at the now defunct Luddenden

Foot railway station. Just across the tiny square a war memorial stands in front of St. Mary's parish church of 1816. Around the back an arched bridge of 1859 crosses Luddenden Brook to the cemetery.

Turn down to the left and over the bridge and take a cobbled path on the right running downstream to a footbridge. Don't cross but take the steps on the left to rise onto a road. Cross at the junction here and take a drive on the right. This runs past a house, a briefly enclosed track emerging into a new housing estate. Until recent times a mill occupied this site. **Keep straight on, the path returning near the end to head off into the woods.** Down below is the brook again, and in between us the long dry former mill-cut downstream from a weir.

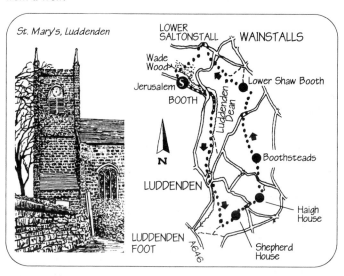

St. Mary's, Luddenden

LOWER SALTONSTALL

WAINSTALLS

Wade Wood

Jerusalem

Lower Shaw Booth

S

BOOTH

Luddenden Dean

N

Boothsteads

LUDDENDEN

Haigh House

LUDDENDEN FOOT

A646

Shepherd House

A fork is quickly reached. The right branch offers five minute's detour as it crosses a side-stream and the mill-cut to an arched footbridge. **Our route takes the upper branch, curving round a gritstone outcrop to a crossroads of paths beneath a flight of steps. Go up the steps to a gap-stile and into the field. Keep straight on to a gate and stile, then over to the top corner beneath the house at Roebucks, ahead. From a corner stile turn up the field-side to a gate above the house and head away up the drive.** Before leaving take a look at the unconventional arrangement of this unsung gem, which dates from 1633.

At once a junction is reached. While the drive goes off right, our way turns up the walled way to the left. Over to the left is Luddenden Foot, a suburban sprawl that long since passed Luddenden in size though not in character: note historic Kershaw House (1650) surviving in amongst incongruous modern development. Beyond, the Calder Valley and Luddenden Dean are divided by Midgley Moor. Just below us, note the interesting roof arrangement at Roebucks. **The track rises and soon levels out to approach the first of several houses at Shepherd House.** These include a 1746 dated house.

Keep straight on the drive, rising to join a road on a hairpin bend. Go left to the next such bend, then take a narrow stone stairway straight up into the wood. When the steps end the thin path turns on to the right, soon winding up through a no-man's-land to reach a gap-stile at the wood top. Go straight up the wall-side, over an old green way and up a crumbling wall-side towards Haigh House. Another fine old house, this dates from 1631 and has yet more mullioned windows.

At the top there is a temptation to go up the left side of the barn, but the right of way currently enters the paddock and goes up between the buildings. Alongside the house, leave the drive and go left up the wall-side on a hollowed way. At a gate at the top rejoin the drive. Go left a few yards only to a gap-stile on the left, and follow the right-hand wall away to emerge onto a road. Luddenden Dean increasingly takes the interest as we forge deeper into it from this contouring route across its eastern flank. **Cross straight over and along the drive opposite which ends at the late 18th century Boothsteads Farm. Don't go round the back of the house but take a gateway on the left yards before it. Keep left of all buildings to enter the field at the back, and head directly away with the wall on the right. After a gateway head on again, but at a tiny kink cross the wall and continue to a stile at the end. This admits onto a rough grassy way. Take the stile opposite to resume with a right-hand wall again.**

This time keep straight on the wall-side to enter a better green lane. Turn down it onto a road, Stocks Lane. Go right past a house and after one field, take a gap-stile on the left. Turn down the wall-side, but on reaching a vestige of a wall above a steeper drop, turn right with it. The views into the finest section of Luddenden Dean are superb. **At the narrowing end cross a fence, hopefully by a new stile and continue on the top of the part wooded bank to curve round to join a rough grassy way. Go left along it to Lower Shaw Booth.** Once again, a splendid old house about 300 years old. In this curious arrangement the central part is most interesting, with an incredible number of mullioned windows strung along the ground floor. **Go straight ahead between the houses and into a field. Bear down to the left along the wall-side, over a stile at the corner and on a thin path towards a house. A stile just above empties onto a hairpin bend of a drive.**

Turn up this to the next such bend, then go straight ahead over a big stone stile. A gem of an embanked little path runs on through several small fields to approach a house at Peace Cote. Ahead, note the little settlement of Lower Saltonstall on the slope in front, an ancient cluster of dark, low houses at one with their surroundings. **Emptying onto the drive, go straight over to a step-stile, and a little path slants down to a road. Again go straight over to a gap-stile, then down a wall-side to the house at Hock Cliff. Pass to its right and head away along the drive. At the road go left to Catywell Bridge and the sudden appearance of the hitherto hidden *Cat-i-th-Well* inn.**

Tucked away on a dead-end road, this popular watering hole is an unashamed corruption of Caty Well, found on the roadside just above the pub. **Continue on from the pub for a minute only to Lower Saltonstall.** In common with neighbouring Upper Saltonstall, this hamlet was a vaccary (cattle farm) run by the Manor of Wakefield 700 years ago. **After the first house on the left turn down a short drive, passing between the houses and down to a gate into a field. Head down the wall-side as far as the first gate/stile on the right, then trace the field-top wall to the next corner. Bear half-left to a gate/stile opposite, from where a faint old path goes diagonally across to a wall-stile. Behind, a little gate admits to the top of Wade Wood.**

This superb deciduous wood comprises largely of birch, oak, beech, holly and much colourful vegetation. **A thin path slants down to the right, working down to a crossroads at a second information board.** This was a junction of ancient tracks from the Saltonstalls towards Midgley. An earlier board tells of the wood's charcoal burning past. **Keep straight on down the thinner path to reach Wade Bridge.** This dates back to the early 19th century, and was rebuilt after flood damage. Its width shows it was meant for the passage of carts rather than mere pedestrian and equestrian use. This charming corner is a place to linger as Luddenden Brook meanders over its stony bed, and especially as the end is only two minutes away! **Cross the bridge and go left up the enclosed green path to return to Jerusalem Farm.**

18

ROBINWOOD

START *Todmorden*   *Grid ref. SD 936241*

DISTANCE *4¼ miles*

ORDNANCE SURVEY MAPS
1:50,000
Landranger 103 - Blackburn & Burnley
1:25,000
Outdoor Leisure 21 - South Pennines

ACCESS *Start from the town centre. There are ample car parks. Todmorden is served by bus and train from Hebden Bridge/Halifax and Rochdale, and by bus from Burnley.*

An exploration of the western valley side running north from Todmorden, featuring woodland, moorland, valley and park.

S First impressions of Todmorden may suggest little obvious charm, but it proves to be a fascinating place with some outstanding buildings. Dobroyd Castle was built in the 1860s for the influential Fielden family, mill owners and local benefactors. The Town Hall was designed by their architect John Gibson in 1875 and features a group of marble figures on a pediment above tall columns. Both the Old Hall and spacious Centre Vale Park are featured along the route. The modest parish church of St. Mary's is centrally sited but tucked away, while the more outgoing Unitarian Church of 1869 boasts a tall spire.

Unlike its counterparts in the valley, which thrived on the woollen industry, Todmorden and its mills were geared to the Lancashire cotton industry; indeed until a century ago Todmorden was quiet literally on the border. Of the three roads heading out, two still aim for the red rose towns of Rochdale and Burnley, both more accessible than Todmorden's Yorkshire masters: a hint of divided loyalties clearly remains hereabouts!

From the roundabout head south on the Rochdale road, and quickly turn up Rise Lane on the right. At once on the left is Todmorden Old Hall, built in 1603 by the Ratcliffe family, who long preceded the Fieldens in Todmorden circles. It features a stunning frontage of gables and mullioned and transomed windows, and is currently a restaurant. **Continue up past the station and under the rail bridge. The road climbs steeply away, but leave it almost at once by the steep Ridge Steps climbing to Well Lane.** Below we have a view over the town viaduct with Stoodley Pike on the skyline. **Turn right and at an early fork bear left on the broad path rising steadily into the trees. Ignoring any lesser branches, this same paths runs all the way on to emerge onto a narrow road, Ewood Lane.** En route Centre Vale Park is outspread below, with views across the valley.

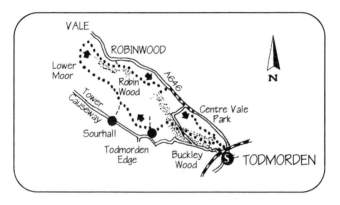

Turn left up the road for 100 yards then take a path on the right, doubling back (partly stepped) to begin a long steady pull up through the wood. At the top is a grand level section before being deposited in a field. The view back over the valley sees the prominent knoll of Whirlaw now topped by higher ground, as well as the Bride Stones, Hawks Stones, the Long Causeway and a glimpse of Coal Clough windfarm. Looking back are Stoodley Pike, Warland Moor and Blackstone Edge. Directly beneath us on the valley floor is the enormous Mons Mill, completely dwarfing the *Hare & Hounds* pub in its shadow. **Go left up the wall-side, becoming enclosed at the end to rise pleasantly to a farm drive at Todmorden Edge.** Todmorden Edge Farm was once a Friends' Meeting House, with a Quaker graveyard alongside.

Go right a short way, and take a gate on the left opposite the last building. Head away along the wall-side, a section being sunken and a little moist. Emerging, don't go on to the far end, but take a gate on the right to resume on the other side of the wall. Over to the right is a rich mix of country, with open moorland patches such as Stannally Stones sat in amongst wall patterned fields. From the gate at the end of the wall, bear left up the field to a gate opposite. Passing through sheep pens a gap-stile admits onto a corner of Lower Moor.

Advance the few yards up onto a drive, and bear right along it past a reedy pool at an old quarry. Ignore the immediate branch down to a house, and keep straight on the track to reach the next house (West End). Passing it, leave the track by slanting up onto the moor. A thin but clear path is found to contour across the moor above the track, passing above another renovated farmhouse of New Towneley and still contouring round to approach the final one. During this a broader path comes in, and they remain the same until above the house (where the track drive finally ends). Here our path also fragments: slant down to join the wall just past the house, and advance on to the corner. A reedy, walled way turns down, soon emerging again to run more happily down to the ruin of Roundfield. Continue down the wall-side to a stile off the bottom of the moor.

Remain with the right-hand wall, which curves round to a promontory above the valley. This is a superb moment with the upper valley at one's feet: the cluster of houses at Vale below, and the wooded Pudsey Clough opposite. This mercurial green path winds around further with the wall to then reveal the view 'down-dale'. It slants superbly down under the rough, craggy flanks of Barewise Wood, faithfully all the way down to the valley floor. En route the *Staff of Life* pub at Robinwood is seen. The path emerges onto a drive at a bridge alongside the road. If the pub door was open, then it's only a minute or two along to the left. The route does not cross onto the road, but turns right along the drive.

At house gates, don't enter the driveway but take a stile by the gate on the right, and a rough path rises away beneath Robin Wood. This improves above a circular pond and runs on beneath a wall to a stile at the end. Look back over the dale to see yet again the great contrast that is Calderdale: Orchan Rocks and Stannally Stones; a mighty railway viaduct and tight packed housing. Two faint old grassy paths head away: take the left-hand one, contouring on through a curious wooded hollow and rising briefly to join a broader green path. Turn down this to a stile into the woods, and a fine path slants down to the rear of Scaitcliff Hall, currently a hotel, then going left down onto the main road at Gate Bottom.

Go right for a couple of minutes, past a school and Ewood Lane to reach the entrance to Central Vale Park. The park was bought from the Fielden family in 1910 for the local population, and features a fine statue of John Fielden, MP for Oldham, who was instrumental in the passing of the 10 Hour Act in 1847, which meant women and children were saved from working more than 10 hours per day! Also here are a War Memorial garden, aviary and aquarium, and enough open space for every family in town.

You can find your own way from here, emerging at the end to continue the final few minutes back into the centre of town. The best option leaves the right-hand far corner of the park, where a path delves into trees behind the cricket club to emerge on a road-end above the sombre Christ Church of 1834. Either keep straight on to rejoin the outward route on Well Lane just short of the finish, or turn down the steps past the church onto the main road.

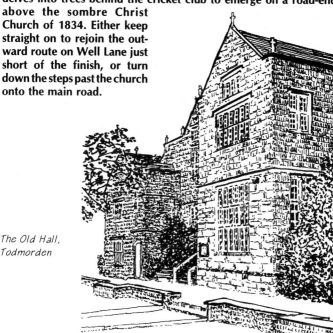

The Old Hall,
Todmorden

19

CRAGG VALE

START Mytholmroyd   Grid ref. SE 012259

DISTANCE 5 miles

ORDNANCE SURVEY MAPS
1:50,000
Landranger 103 - Blackburn & Burnley
          104 - Leeds, Bradford & Harrogate
1:25,000
Outdoor Leisure 21 - South Pennines

ACCESS Start from the village centre. There is a small car park just over the bridge at the main T-junction. Served by Halifax-Hebden Bridge buses and trains.

A moderately strenuous but outstanding walk savouring the charm of Cragg Vale, the over-riding feature being its many wooded delights.

S Mytholmroyd is the quieter, poor relation of Hebden Bridge, little more than a mile distant. It sprang up with the textile mills, and now large pockets of modern housing extend on both sides of the valley. St. Michael's church stands just across the river, where the major side valley of Cragg Vale joins the Calder. Such is the reputation of the local dock leaves that Mytholmroyd is home of a restored tradition, the World Dock Pudding Championship.

Cross the bridge on the B6138, along New Road passing under the railway bridge. On the left is the modern Roman Catholic church of the Good Shepherd. **Opposite the *Shoulder of Mutton* (note the mounting steps) bear left on Scout Road.** Just on the left here note an old house with its mullioned windows. **At once turn sharply right up Hall Bank Lane at the side of the Methodist Church. Remain on this road as it makes a quick exit from town to country.** Free of the houses we look down over Mytholmroyd to the moors behind. Heptonstall church tower is conspicuous on the skyline, while over Cragg Vale, Bell House Moor and Broadhead Clough look splendid, more so as the walk progresses. **The road winds up to suddenly end as a drive bears off to the left.**

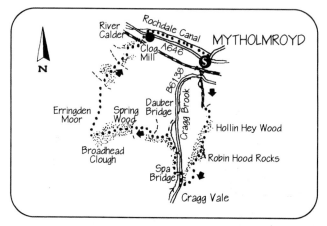

Our continuation of Stake Lane is the enclosed footpath directly ahead, climbing partly flagged and setted through colourful vegetation. Part way up, leave at a stile by a gate on the right, and a green path runs along the wall-side beneath myriad holly trees. Half-way along, bear left up a grassy way which rises faintly to an old wall corner, then on behind a small outbuilding. A broader track then slants up through the scattered trees to a gate at the top. Don't go through, but take the path on the right which commences a grand walk along the top of Hollin Hey Wood. The inspection lids marked 'MWW' indicate that we are on the line of an aqueduct constructed by Morley Water Works to supply the town from the reservoir it built at Withens Clough across Cragg Vale in 1894.

At the end the path emerges into more open country. Revealed are outstanding views over Cragg Vale, with little urbanisation left to impinge. Finest features are the wealth of woodland, and the prospect of the wooded bowl of Broadhead Clough opposite, our return route. **The path advances to a seat above a rash of crags, a fine spot to halt. Just past here it dips down, and the main path slants down to the right.** Just ahead a thinner 'non right of way' path continues onto the crest of the larger Robin Hood Rocks.

Our descending path quickly swings left, and avoiding lesser branches runs on (with glimpses to the rocks above) to a stile out of the wood. Cross the field to the gateway ahead and turn down the near-side of the wall to a gate and stile. Continue on a clear path down to the edge of the wood, then bear left down a causeyed, walled way to a row of houses in Cragg Vale. Turn down to the right here, and at the houses below go right on a path dropping down onto the road.

Cragg Vale from Robin Hood Rocks

Go right on the footway for a minute or two, then at the first chance turn down a drive to Spa Bridge on Cragg Brook. Across, take a stile on the right from where a path turns downstream. This is only a permissive path, and walkers are requested to keep exactly to it in this conservation area. **A lovely, wooded walk leads down to Clough Foot Bridge: just up to the left another stile gives access to a meadow, crossing it to resume downstream in woodland. The path soon swings left to a footbridge over a tiny brook, then rises onto a drive.** For an easy return, turn right down this to Dauber Bridge, from where the starting point is only half a mile distant along the road.

For part two of the walk, turn left up the drive rising alongside the wooded clough. At the end it forks: bear left, a good track running on to appraise the great skyline of Bell Hole. On entering Spring Wood the drive forks. Take neither, but go straight ahead along a much more inviting path. Here we enter Broadhead Clough Nature Reserve, run by the Yorkshire Wildlife Trust. Please stick to the path.

The delightful path winds on and gradually upwards into the deep confines of this glorious woodland. Towards the top a fence comes in on the right and the birch trees thin out to be replaced by bracken: look out for a stile in it when a fainter path keeps straight on. Above the stile a surprise awaits, for within a few feet the path climbs to the rim of the amphitheatre, the climbing is finished. A tall stake serves as a useful waymark for those locating the start of the path from above. The great natural hollow of Broadhead Clough is also known locally as Bell Hole: this is truly a place to linger.

Resume by crossing the few yards to the crumbling wall corner behind, and head off along a path down its long length across Erringden Moor. At the end a wall corner is reached. Go left to another corner, then trace a faint trod bearing left across the corner of the moor, crossing quickly to a stile in a fence. Pass through the crumbling wall behind and start the long descent, the first section being alongside a long abandoned hollowed way. The valley floor quickly appears outspread below.

The old way leads down to a firm track. Go right a few yards then resume the descent on a path slanting back to the left. This proves a splendid route down the hillside, for our way remains uncultivated virtually all the way. **The path runs down towards a pylon, just beneath which it swings left, more defined towards the edge of the trees. Without entering fully it turn downhill again, through some trees and later slanting right to a stile onto a drive, with a house just along to the left.**

Cross straight over down a thin path alongside a wooded stream. Emerging, continue down the field-side to a single slab footbridge at a tiny confluence. Now bear left across the field to a prominent gate in front of the trees. A walled track is joined, and this leads down to the right. Bear left at the bottom, the road becoming surfaced to cross railway and river and emerge onto the main road alongside a tall mill. This is the home of Walkley Clogs, where you can actually study the clog making process with great interest. Today it has blossomed into a sizeable tourist attraction, and there are craft and gift shops and a cafe on the premises.

Cross the road with extreme caution to join the towpath of the Rochdale Canal. For more on the canal, see page 41. **Turn right for a short walk back into Mytholmroyd. Passing a lock and a couple of stone arched bridges, leave the towpath at steps up to a modern road bridge. Turn right down Midgley Road to finish.**

20

BLACK HAMELDON

START *Widdop*   *Grid ref. SD 946323*

DISTANCE *8½ miles*

ORDNANCE SURVEY MAPS
1:50,000
Landranger 103 - Blackburn & Burnley
1:25,000
Outdoor Leisure 21 - South Pennines

ACCESS *Start from a parking area half a mile west of the Pack Horse, where the Gorple reservoir road leaves the Heptonstall-Colne road.*

A walk through Noah Dale and an at times rough march along the Pennine watershed, brightened up by a set of moorland reservoirs. Not recommended in poor weather, the top being rather featureless.

•*IMPORTANT* Much of this walk is on permissive paths on Yorkshire Water land or an access area of North West Water.

❸ **From the lay-by take the gate across the road and head off along the reservoir road to the dam of Gorple Lower Reservoir.** Along with its higher neighbour it was completed in 1934. **Turn along it, and at the end go left on the reservoir road to the isolated Gorple Cottages. Just beyond them the Pennine Way is met. Follow it on the broad track up to the right, bridging a reservoir drain and rising up the moor. When the PW goes off to the left, remain on the track over the brow of Heptonstall Moor.**

Whilst climbing, a quarry site is passed on the right, where stone was won for the reservoir construction. Ahead from the brow a sweeping Calderdale skyline is dominated by the monument on Stoodley Pike. Down in front is the Colden Valley, the upper section we are about to descend to being known as Noah Dale. On the moor to the right, just two minutes away, the conspicuous Reaps Cross is worth a detour. Possibly dating from medieval times, it stands astride an old moorland packway, though sadly its upper section has been broken off.

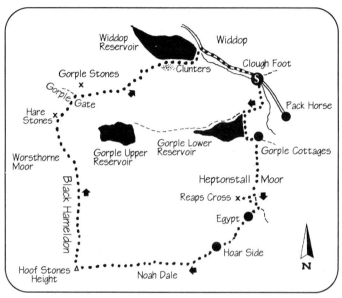

The track runs quickly down to a gate off the moor. Don't follow the rough road away, but take a stile on the right and follow the drive to the renovated house at Egypt. The track runs on past it to drop down to Rough Hey, surely beyond redemption? A gap-stile in the corner beneath the ruin gives access to a path down to a footbridge in a tiny clough. From the small gate above, a thin but clear path bears left, contouring round the pasture (again part-flagged) to run on to a crumbling wall. The path continues to a stile in a solid wall to approach the house at Hoar Side. Keep left of the grounds, and on past the house (part flagged) to a small gate below a larger one in the corner ahead.

What follows is an interesting lesson in dereliction. **A path drops down to a solitary building (once Colden Water Farm) by the beck just ahead, then rises away from it between old walls. This same old track, hollowed between crumbling walls, leads unfailingly on**

above the bank. Ignoring a branch down to a bridge it starts to slant up again, rising above the ruins of two further farms, Pad Laithe and Noah Dale. The remains of mullioned windows suggest the latter was a house of some character. Ahead, meanwhile, the breached Noah Dale dam appears. **Above these second ruins the way ends, and a stile admits onto the rough moor.** From here the path is waymarked all the way to the top.

Continue along the old wall and fence side as far as the wall corner, where the path bears left to the end of the former dam wall. The dam built in this lonely spot was probably to serve mills down the valley, though there were also lead mines in the vicinity. Though long since burst the remains show it to have been quite substantial. Vegetation has returned to the extent that the old retaining wall is the only evidence of the old reservoir. **The thin path runs on the near side of the old reservoir, and rises gently up the slope at the other end. A grassy ditch is soon joined and proves a perfect route up the easing slopes to gain the watershed on Black Hameldon.**

At 1571ft this highest point of Black Hameldon is known as Hoof Stones Height, and is occupied by an Ordnance Survey column (S4491). It is the joint highest point in Calderdale, and the highest point attained in this collection of walks. It is surrounded by a modest scattering of rock, but the big surprise is the startling appearance of the very near Coal Clough windfarm on the Long Causeway just below. Otherwise, the surrounds are almost exclusively moorland. Here the permissive path from Noah Dale dam ends, and we trace the boundary of North West Water's Worsthorne Moor access area all the way along the skyline as far as the Gorple Gate.

Turn right along the broad watershed, a peaty path tracing the old boundary ditch. To the west is all Lancashire, dominated by the bulk of Pendle Hill. **A good mile of undulating terrain leads to the northerly 'top' at 1525ft before a pronounced descent.** This offers a lovely stride, with grand open views: just down to the left is Cant Clough Reservoir. **An improved section of grassy ditch leads down to the saddle. The ditch ends here, and a path rises past the modest grouping of the Hare Stones to quickly join Gorple Gate.** There is not actually a gate here, of course, for 'gate' is an old name for a track or pathway. Gorple Gate is a historic way over the moors from Worsthorne in Lancashire, and was an important trans-Pennine packhorse route three centuries ago, lime and cloth being major goods. Just down to the right now is Gorple Upper Reservoir.

Immediately above are the major scattering of boulders known as the Gorple Stones, while down to the right is all that remains of what was the particularly isolated farmhouse of Gorple. **Turn right along the track which runs pleasantly on to a point above the substantial outcrops of Shuttleworth Moor before commencing a gentle descent.** Widdop Reservoir appears in its entirety ahead, backed by an impressive line of crags. The reservoir was built by Halifax Corporation and completed in 1878, over 50 years before the walk's two earlier reservoirs, and almost equals their joint capacity. Materials reached the site by means of a 5½ mile long horse-drawn tramway from further down the valley.

Reaps Cross, looking north to Gorple, Walshaw and Widdop

Simply remain on the track as it zigzags steeply down before running on beneath a plantation and along the reservoir side. The trees were an experimental plantation shortly after world war two, but did not prove a roaring success. Up to the right immediately after the trees are the impressive rock formations of Cludders, of which the finest buttress almost overhangs the very corner of the dam. Not surprisingly, many challenging and easily accessible rock climbs are recorded here, though the north facing aspect and relative high altitude deter many modern climbers. **Cross the dam to the road and turn right for an easy stroll past Clough Foot to the start.** Shortly after leaving the dam, look back over your right shoulder to see a giant 'rocking' stone perched on one of the crags on the moor edge.

21

BLACKSTONE EDGE

START *Baitings*   *Grid ref. SD 999186*

DISTANCE *8½ miles*

ORDNANCE SURVEY MAPS
1:50,000
Landranger 109 - Manchester
*   110 - Sheffield & Huddersfield (tiny section)*
1:25,000
Outdoor Leisure 21 - South Pennines

ACCESS *Start from the large roadside parking area to the west of Baitings Reservoir. Served by Halifax-Rochdale buses.*

A bracing walk through archetypal South Pennine moorland. Much of the walk, however, is on easy paths and tracks, though not to be underestimated as it does cross fairly wild moorland. As far as the M62, the walk is on Yorkshire Water permissive paths, some of which are on the urban common of Rishworth Moor. The dominant feature is the presence of the hand of man, in the shape of reservoirs, roads, motorways, Roman road, packways, pylons, windfarms, drains....

❺ Head back along the road towards Baitings, passing Blue Ball Road then taking the unsignposted road right. This runs down to cross the upper reach of Baitings Reservoir by means of Baitings Viaduct. Baitings Reservoir was completed as recently as 1956 on the site of a much smaller reservoir dating from the 1920s. It now fills a vast area of the broader, upper reaches of the Ryburn Valley. From the viaduct in times of low water levels, the bridge and old road that ran above the original reservoir are revealed. Over to the left the reservoir itself appears above the trees, with the white walled *Blue Ball Inn* prominent on the slope behind.

Remain on the road up to the very brow to reach Yorkshire Water's Heights car park. Here turn up to the right on a wall-side track across a patch of rough moor. This quickly becomes enclosed to run pleasantly on to emerge onto a corner of Rishworth Moor. Continue on the wall-side track. As the wall turns away, advance up the moor on a clearly defined sunken way. A path shadows it, served intermittently by marker posts. Our way was hollowed by the passage of sleds of quarried stone being brought down off the moor. Over to the right beyond Manshead End, Stoodley Pike appears, itself overtopped on a clear day by Boulsworth Hill.

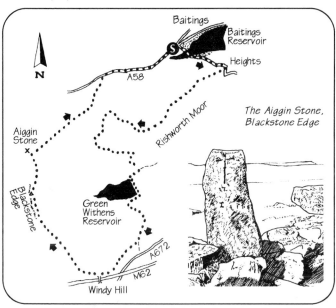

The path rises gently for some time, then the sunken way begins to falter. Markers send the thin path along to the right: it is more prominent just ahead, as a broader green way. This rises gently to a junction just short of the brow. Here turn to the right to commence a long, level trod in the company of a reedy drain that quickly forms. Warm Withens Drain now remains our way for a good stride. Ahead is a vast array of pylons backed by the moors north of Littleborough and across the Walsden Gorge, then distant Pendle Hill directly behind the Coal Clough windfarm.

The drain path curves sharply back round to the left. Just ahead Blackstone Edge is seen from the 'back', and further left the Windy Hill mast. **The drain is vacated at a junction with the concrete Rishworth Drain. Go left here, but instead of the more obvious path with the main drain, go left on a thin path alongside a minor channel.** This 'nick' in the moor reveals the M62 motorway and the moors to the south: Green Withens Reservoir also appears below. **A clearer way runs on with the drain to Green Withens Edge. The waymarked point of departure is in any case obvious as it comes at the sudden demise of the drain. Turn down the moor and bear left on the path crossing to a broad bridge over another major drain. Turn right on the wide track to quickly reach the dam of Green Withens Reservoir.**

March along the dam and around to the waterworks building on the other side. All the while, Blackstone Edge features prominently across the rising moor beyond the head of the reservoir. Green Withens Reservoir was completed in 1898 by Wakefield Corporation, and enlarged in 1925. **At the track junction go left on the main drive out, yet again with a drain for company.** The M62 appears seemingly yards in front: very soon it will be, literally! **When the reservoir road turns off for the main road, remain on a green track by the drain to reach its terminus at a basin under the motorway fence. Turn up its side to reach the Pennine Way footbridge.**

Though we don't cross it, many will take this chance to be the highest person in the country 'on' a motorway. **Joining the PW therefore, bear right on the broad path heading away, soon swinging around to the right to replace the M62 with the prospect of Blackstone Edge, a fair deal!** This splendidly restored path will be a major shock to anyone unaware of it, for its predecessor across the peat bogs of Redmires is but a distant memory. **With the bouldery crest of the edge straight ahead, the path leads unerringly up to its top. The edge itself actually forms well before the waymarked path reaches it, and many obviously make for its attractions when the path is just yards short of the edge. At 1548ft the highest point is not in doubt, as Ordnance Survey column S4502 is cemented securely to a mighty boulder.**

This is the second highest point in this collection of Calderdale walks, being overtopped only by Black Hameldon in the preceding walk. The view is truly outstanding, though perhaps the finest feature is the rocky edge itself. Westwards we look down on a great spread of Mancunia beyond Littleborough and Hollingworth Lake. The Summit Gorge leads the eye to Coal Clough windfarm and Pendle Hill through the Cliviger Gorge, while to the north Black Hameldon and Boulsworth Hill lead round to Ovenden Moor windfarm. Southwards, meanwhile, are the high moors of the Dark Peak. The finest climbing ground amongst what is otherwise largely scrambling opportunities is found towards the northern limits of the edge, and set a short way down the slope: this proves to be a massive cliff with bold faces and one or two interesting chimneys.

Resume northwards along the edge path (marker posts throughout), soon crossing more modest stony ground to a gate admitting onto the old road at the Aiggin Stone. This is a junction of once important packhorse routes, where the Rochdale-Halifax and Oldham-Burnley trails met. The old guide stone has been restored, and remarkably there is more of it below ground than above. Further down the Lancashire side is the superb surviving cobbled section, long attributed to the Romans but almost certainly dating from packhorse times.

Turn right, the path crossing the brow and soon shaking off the fence. A gradual descent begins on a broad, grassy, part sunken way, to reach a crossroads with a drain and attendant path. Continue straight down, the broad way quickly resuming and enjoying a section where paving has remained uncovered by the vegetation of the dormant years. At the bottom Rag Sapling Clough is joined. Turn left with the stream, the path now thin and occasionally moist, but again enjoying some paved sections to approach the A58. Ahead, Manshead End offers a shapely profile.

After a grassy bridge over a side stream just short of the road, the old path slants along to the right to pass beneath the prominent retaining wall before meeting the road. This is one of the quieter main roads. Turn down for ten minutes, passing a line of old quarries and using patchy verges to complete the walk.

Blackstone Edge

22
BLACK BROOK

START *Stainland*   *Grid ref. SE 078195*

DISTANCE *4¾ miles*

ORDNANCE SURVEY MAPS
1:50,000
Landranger 104 - Leeds, Bradford & Harrogate
*   110 - Sheffield & Huddersfield*
1:25,000
Outdoor Leisure 21 - South Pennines

ACCESS *Start from the village centre. The main street has a car park.*
Served by Halifax-Elland-Huddersfield buses, or directly from Halifax.

An exploration of the unsung side valley of Black Brook, with the
ancient settlement of Barkisland as the midway point.

S Stainland is a hilltop community equidistant from Halifax and
Huddersfield. The village lost its railway from Greetland in 1959.
Several of its features are mentioned at the start and finish of the route.
**Head eastwards along the main street a short way and turn left along
Drury Lane just yards after the Post office and Holroyd Square.**
Beginning as a short-lived cobbled street, Drury Lane was made for
carting stone from the quarries at the other end. **It continues as a
walled path running past allotments and between the fields. At the
end it emerges suddenly onto a brow above a line of old quarries at
Eaves Top.** This is a splendid viewpoint, looking over the great sprawl
of Halifax and its neighbourhood. **Go left on the main track slanting
down onto a grassy sward beneath large quarried cliffs.**

**Level with a large free-standing boulder, go right to the edge of the
bank where a distinct footpath turns away. This doubles back down
the slope between old retaining walls. Within a minute bear left at
a guidepost to descend to the top of the golf course.** Warning signs
tell you what action to take if someone yells 'fore!'. **Go straight down,**

passing right of a large patch of trees and down to the nearest trees below. A path runs down through them to escape the golf course. Continue down the wooded bank to emerge by a stile into a field. Bear left down to the bottom to emerge by a row of houses in the shadow of a derelict mill at Gate Head.

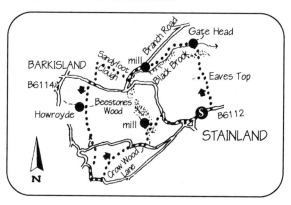

Cross the bridge beyond and turn immediately upstream on a thin path shadowing Black Brook. The transition into rural surrounds is very sudden. Note the old mill-cut wall opposite, a curious construction with vertically placed stones incorporated. Stick to the beck to approach the mill ahead, this old path bearing across the field to enter another derelict millyard. Keep straight on through the buildings and up its access road at the end to join the Branch Road.

Go left on the footway until just past a bend, then take a narrow stile immediately after the lone house on the right. After its garden wall ends bear right up to the field corner. From the gate head straight up the side of tree-lined Sandyfoot Clough. The path ends with a stile in the adjacent fence and no obvious way ahead. Rise by a crumbling wall to a wall corner above, and on past a shed to enter a walled track. At the end don't go right into the modern housing, but take a gap-stile by the gate in front to enter the drive of Barkisland Hall. This is a real gem, dating from 1638 and flaunting a magnificent three storeyed front. Its short drive leads out onto Stainland Road at the foot of Barkisland. Turn up into the main street. Our point of departure is a narrow gap-stile on the left, immediately after the village stocks at the second house. Just yards up the street are a rather splendid house and just above, the *Griffin Inn*, both on the right.

Departing, a short snicket leaves the stile to enter a field. **Descend with the wall to Barkisland Clough, crossing a single slab bridge and up some stone steps out of the trees. Head away with the wall to run along to an old green lane.** The house hidden on the right is Howroyde, which dates from 1642. **Cross straight over, now with a wall on the right. At the end go on to another wall just ahead, then accompany another right-hand wall. From the stile at the end, bear left to the far corner in front of the farm buildings.** Directly ahead the traffic of the M62 can be seen. **From the gate a short-lived walled way runs on into the yard.** Pause to admire the old house with its mullioned and transomed windows. **Opposite the house, leave the drive by a gap-stile on the left and cross the field to the top of wooded Bottomley Clough. A stile admits onto a lane.**

Go left a few yards then take a stile on the right. At the field-end stile a part-paved pathway is crossed. From the next stile ahead keep straight on along the bottom of several narrow fields, with gap-stiles all the way. At the end a longer field leads on to join a short drive, which leads out onto Steel Lane. Turn downhill, and at the second cobbled bend go left on a broad path through rough pasture. As an inviting green path it slants briefly up to a corner stile. With the path gone, cross the field top towards a derelict farm. Keeping left enter a green lane, passing round the back of the house and out on its old drive. As a smashing green track (Crow Wood Lane) it runs down to emerge onto another hairpin bend. Turn down above a millpond to the valley floor, occupied by a vast board mill.

Rising away, turn left at the first chance on an access road on the top side of the mill. Just before it turns left, take an inviting green path doubling back to the right. This old way rises into trees and enjoys a superb zigzag climb through the wood to emerge up a short walled way. At the top go left on the wall-side to the foot of an access drive (Broad Royd). Turn up past the short terrace to join Beestonley Lane. Go right up the footway to re-enter Stainland.

Views over to the right lead up the Black Brook valley to the M62 crossing the Scammonden dam. En route the old Providence Chapel of 1814 is passed: this massive building has been converted into dwellings. **Keep on, bearing left at a couple of junctions to return to the start.** On the first of these the house on the left corner at Well Royd bears a 1762 datestone. Several pubs are passed, along with the old farmhouse of Ellistones with its mullioned windows.

23

EDGE END MOOR

START *Hebden Bridge*   *Grid ref. SD 991272*

DISTANCE *4¾ miles*

ORDNANCE SURVEY MAPS
1:50,000
Landranger 103 - Blackburn & Burnley
1:25,000
Outdoor Leisure 21 - South Pennines

ACCESS *Start from the town centre. Ample car parks. Served by Halifax-Todmorden buses and trains.*

Delightful woodlands sandwich a bright stroll on a shelf high above the valley, encircling Edge End Moor in the shadow of Stoodley Pike.

S As self-proclaimed 'South Pennine Centre', Hebden Bridge is the focal point for this set of walks. It is for here that most of the modern 'tourists' make, partly for its position at the foot of the famous Hebden Dale (universally Hardcastle Crags), but also for its own attractions. Its houses climb alarmingly up the steep hillsides above the meeting of the valleys, while in and near the lively centre are canal trips, a packhorse bridge, a clog factory, collectors' shops and an invaluable information centre.

From the Tourist Information Centre cross the road and along Holme Street past the Post office to gain the canal towpath. Cross the stone arched bridge at Blackpit Lock and turn right along the canal bank. At once this is carried over the river Calder by the Black Pit Aqueduct of 1797. **The path quickly turns off, up some steps then along to the right to meet a road. Go left here, through pedestrian lights on the railway bridge and uphill. Turn up the rough drive behind the first row of houses on the right. Half way up, leave this by a more inviting walled path doubling back up to the right.** Here savour possibly the finest bird's-eye view of the town, with the Colden and Hebden valleys striking away behind. **At a wall, turn left on a thinner path rising into Crow Nest Wood. At the top a stile empties onto a broad lane, with a mast just to the left. Cross straight over and up the field-sides, soon reaching the brow whereupon virtually all the climbing is already done.** Ahead, Stoodley Pike appears.

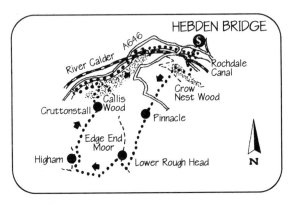

Maintain this course along several field-sides to meet a road. Cross straight over and along Pinnacle Lane. Pinnacle Farm is quickly passed, an attractive house with mullioned windows, dating from the 17th century. **Again, just keep straight on this aptly named lane with the Stoodley Pike monument directly ahead. Sections of causey occupy a short length, appropriately at a moist section. Eventually this green lane emerges into a field, with Lower Rough Head Farm just across to the right. Continue on two field-sides further to empty onto a rough farm lane. Turn right towards the farm.**

Level with the house, don't turn right on its drive heading away, but take a stile on the left. An embanked path runs along the wall-side, again bound for the monument. At the end a tract of rough moor is entered. Cross straight over on a faint path to meet a stile where wall and fence meet ahead. Don't cross it, but turn right on an old green track with the fence. The monument looms highly above now, while Todmorden and its environs appear on the dale floor. **The track soon starts to slant down the wall-side as a sunken way. Towards the bottom a farm (Height Gate) is seen just below. Here bear around to the right on a contouring path, the idea being to keep above the various buildings spread below.**

Maintain this contour, meeting a broader green way marked by white stones, passing above a ruined barn and then the house at Higham. After doubling back out above the minor clough above it, the path starts a gradual descent. Quickly take a thinner path branching right, contouring gently round again (well above the house at Lodge) to run on to a gate. Through it keep straight on the fence side along the base of Edge End Moor. This course is held for some time now, an easy stroll on a clear path. After an accompanying wall departs, the ruined house of Cruttonstall is seen ahead. Part way across, fork left towards it. A short, walled track leads along past the buildings. With its mullioned windows this was clearly a house of substance many decades ago.

At the end of the field the old drive heads away between more crumbling walls to the top of Callis Wood. A stile gives access, and a zigzag descent begins. This proves to be a smashing old track, well made with retaining walls. There are two hairpins, the second being a touch less obvious as it doubles back right just above fields at the edge of the wood. Somewhat overgrown, this lower section runs on to meet a firm drive. Turn down this, passing Callis Wood Farm and zigzagging down to bridge the canal at Callis Wood Bottom. Here join the towpath and follow it all the way back to the start. En route we pass the *Stubbing Wharf* pub, several locks and almost at the end Hebble End, featuring a cafe, crafts, and the World of the Honeybee, an interesting attraction very popular with the younger end.

Hebden Bridge

MANSHEAD HILL

START *Baitings*   *Grid ref. SE 012190*

DISTANCE *5½ miles*

ORDNANCE SURVEY MAPS
1:50,000
Landranger 103 - Blackburn & Burnley
104 - Leeds, Bradford & Harrogate
109 - Manchester
110 - Sheffield & Huddersfield
1:25,000
Outdoor Leisure 21 - South Pennines

ACCESS *Start from the Yorkshire water car park at Baitings Dam on the A58 west of Ripponden. Served by Halifax-Rochdale buses.*

A richly varied walk dominated by a cracking moorland crossing of a magnificent viewpoint. The path over Manshead Hill is a permissive one created in partnership with Yorkshire Water.

S Baitings Reservoir was completed in 1956 on the site of a smaller dam dating from the 1920s. It now fills a vast area of the upper reaches of the Ryburn Valley. The massive concrete dam might rapidly induce vertigo, being curiously sinuous and with unusually low walls. Hold on to your false teeth if brave enough to peer over it! The roadside *New Inn* displays the interesting appendage of a large sundial.

Cross the dam and head up the track opposite to Upper Schole Carr Farm. Pass to the right of the house and up the drive onto a road. Looking back, shapely Manshead End projects itself invitingly above the reservoir, which is largely screened by trees. **Turn right, descending to cross Baitings Viaduct.** This bridges the upper reach of the reservoir. From it, in times of low water levels, the bridge and old road that ran above the original reservoir are revealed. **The road then rises to join the A58. Go left past a junction with Blue Ball Road, then within a minute go right to a stile at the start of the permissive path up Manshead Hill.**

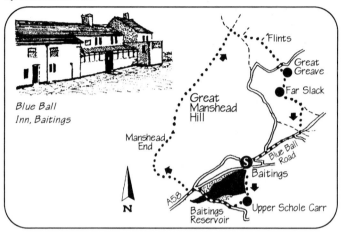

Blue Ball Inn, Baitings

Flints

Great Greave

Far Slack

Great Manshead Hill

Manshead End

Blue Ball Road

Baitings

N

A58

Baitings Reservoir

Upper Schole Carr

The path drops to cross a stream then works its way up the side of Greenwood Clough. Passing left of the old farm at Manshead, it re-crosses the stream and bears left through a gap-stile. Part way up the rough enclosure pass through a gap in the crumbling wall to access a step-stile in a fence. The clear path now rises over open moor, aided throughout by regular posts. Soon the upper reach of the clough is re-crossed, an old wall passed through and the path rises to the waiting edge of Manshead End. The final pull is a short, stiff one to a waiting cairn. This is the finest moment of the walk, and the modest rash of stones is the perfect venue for a refreshment halt.

Just beyond, the path runs on to a sturdy shelter cairn and an Ordnance Survey column (S4404). At 1368ft this is the summit of Great Manshead Hill. The all round panorama is quite superb. Westwards is layer upon layer of rolling moorland; features across the Summit Gorge such as Freeholds Top, coming round to Stoodley Pike monument, Coal Clough windfarm on the Long Causeway, the Gorple and Widdop moors, Ovenden Moor windfarm, Norland Moor, and then round by way of Emley Moor TV mast behind

Ringstone Edge Reservoir towards Baitings Reservoir, with the moors beyond supporting Holme Moss TV mast at the northern limits of the Peak National Park. **The path continues north along the hill, keeping generally left of the watershed.** This has the advantage of views down into the colourful upper reaches of Cragg Vale. Ahead, Sowerby Bridge adds an urban touch to this varied scene.

Eventually a wall comes in below, and the path drops down to join a track alongside it. The first of several 'S B' boundary stones within the next half-mile is passed. **Continue on to a crossroads of tracks and turn right past a red brick ruin.** This is part of the scant remains of a wartime decoy site, meant to confuse German bombers. **At a wall-corner leave by a stile. The path is guided across a rough enclosure to the corner of the old Flints Reservoir, then runs along the right-hand embankment to join a track at a bend. Turn down this, soon becoming fully enclosed to debouch onto a narrow road.**

Go right for a minute and down the first drive. At the bend, go straight through the big gates into the yard of Great Greave. This proves to be a grand old house, tucked away from the outside world. Dating from the early 17th century, its hidden frontage boasts two gables, mullioned windows and a superb outlook. **Pass round to the right and without going to the front, turn through a small gap by a shed and descend an overgrown old way.** This is not recommended in shorts in high summer! **This drops down between walls into Blackshaw Clough. Escape into the field opposite and head up the wall-side. At the stile above, turn to admire Great Greave.**

Continue up the wall-side to Far Slack Farm. Squeeze through a gap left of the first building to emerge into the yard, and follow the drive straight out. At a junction of tracks at the next house, turn up the more inviting walled green way on the right. This winds most pleasantly up to emerge onto a road. **Turn right along the quiet Blue Ball Road with excellent views for a good three-quarters of a mile to reach the *Blue Ball Inn*.** This popular hostelry is an old packhorse inn serving the route out of Lancashire over Blackstone Edge proper (see WALK 21). This was superseded by the modern turnpike road over Blackstone Edge which adopted the lower route by the pub's suitably named lower neighbour. The *Blue Ball* has a reputation for its choice of ales and its view over the dam to Rishworth Moor. A short verse adorns the wall above the door. **Leave the road in front of the pub and descend to the *New Inn* below, and thus conclude the walk.**

25

OVENDEN MOOR

START *Ogden*   *Grid ref. SE 066309*

DISTANCE *5 miles*

ORDNANCE SURVEY MAPS
1:50,000
Landranger 104 - Leeds, Bradford & Harrogate
1:25,000
*Outdoor Leisure 21 - South Pennines **or** Pathfinder 682 - Bradford*

ACCESS *Start from the Yorkshire Water car park at Ogden Water, on Ogden Lane just off the A629 at Causeway Foot. Served by Halifax-Denholme-Keighley and Halifax-Thornton-Bradford buses.*

⑤ Ogden Reservoir was built by Halifax Corporation in 1858. In recent years it has been renamed Ogden Water, and improved access features woodland paths and an easy circuit of the reservoir. There is an information booth (seasonally manned) and toilets. **At the far end of the lower car park a kissing-gate admits into the trees.** Children in particular will delight in seeking out several wooden carvings in the plantation. **While one path drops straight down to the reservoir shore, a good path also runs straight ahead, only slowly nearing the foot of the wood. At the end it approaches the head of the reservoir and meets a broader track coming down from the right. Down to the left the reservoir side path runs along to a bridge over a tiny side dam.**

Our way, however, resumes along the track, which quickly narrows into a path to forge pleasantly on above the lively beck. The end of the wood is soon reached, and from the stile a clear path runs on through the open country of Ogden Clough. This steep walled clough is a little gem, and the beckside path soon reaches a twin set of waterfalls. Here the peaty moorland stream tumbles over uniform gritstone ledges. **At the second falls the path rises up to a junction alongside a sturdy bridge over another little dam.**

91

Immediately upstream are sizeable gritstone crags. **Across the bridge a path rises away, running to a stile onto Ovenden Moor.** At this point the wind turbines make their first appearance, looming alarmingly just ahead! **A clear path heads away towards them, rising imperceptibly to a brow.** The turbines are now almost within touching distance, while just ahead the *Withens Hotel* appears. **The path drops down to bridge the upper reaches of Skirden Clough then rises as a broader track to meet the firm track of Withens New Road. For a quick return go left, otherwise turn right for two minutes to the beckoning pub.**

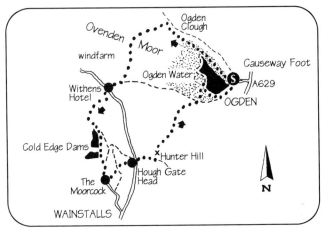

The *Withens Hotel* was built in 1862 to serve quarrymen, and is the highest pub in West Yorkshire. A five minute detour along the road leads to an information area at the windfarm. You will discover that these 23 wind turbines are 100ft high and can power 7,500 homes. Try to calculate how many would be needed to supply Calderdale: you'd certainly need an alternative activity to rambling anyway, because there wouldn't be any room left on the moor for you and me!

To resume, cross straight over the road from the pub and down a walled track. This swings left then down to the right to a group of semi-ruinous farm buildings. The track goes right a few yards at the end of these, then runs firmly along towards another abandoned farmhouse. Passing this, the track swings left to approach the Cold Edge Dams. Just short of the first one, Haigh Cote Dam, branch off to join a thin path along the embankment. Follow this to the far end of the main embankment. The path then crosses a little tract of

heather moorland to do likewise on the smaller Leadbeater Dam. At the first corner, however, turn down to join a track and head away with it. As it approaches a fence go straight ahead to locate a corner stile down below, admitting back onto the broad track left earlier.

Go right a minute or so, absorbing the Calderdale Way for the next half-mile through the fields. Immediately after the first buildings on the left turn into the yard. This proves to be the *Moorcock*, an isolated and historic pub barely recognisable as such! At the corner near the building a stile admits to a field. Cross the centre to the next stile, then straight on a narrow way. This leads to a flagged field-side path onto a walled track. Go left a matter of yards then take a stile on the right. Cross straight over the field to a tiny plank footbridge, then up the wall-side. After a ladder-stile take a stile behind to a thin path up the other side of the wall. At the top the diverted path goes round the left side of Hough Gate Head Farm, and up the field to join its drive. A few yards above it rejoins Cold Edge Road.

Once again go left a few yards only then take a gate on the right. A broad, part-flagged track heads away. After a spell between walls it swings gently right, descending steadily into an old quarried area at Hunter Hill. Ahead is a sweeping prospect over the northern Halifax suburbs. The Calderdale Way heads into the heart of this varied scene, but we must part company. At a crossroads of tracks the Calderdale Way prepares to become enclosed again: here take the inviting branch left towards a couple of trees. The low ruins in their shadow are all that remains of Slaughter Gap. This was named after a Civil War skirmish in 1644, when Parliamentarian troops came off worst.

After the last ruin a trod contours across the pasture to a kissing-gate back onto a corner of Ovenden Moor. Follow the right-hand wall away until it turns off, then advance on a thin path to the edge of a slope. A golf course occupies the colourful hollow below. The path descends to a stile onto the course, then a couple of marker posts send us across, bearing gently left to a bridge over the central stream. Almost at once a path slants up the slope alongside a bracken patch, bearing right on the brow and sent via markers to join the Withens New Road again in front of the plantation.

While the track leads quickly down to the dam, a nicer finish takes the stile in front. A good track runs down through the trees towards the reservoir wall. When it swings left to climb away, take a gap in the wall to join the reservoir path. Turn right along here to the dam and cross it to finish.

SOME USEFUL ADDRESSES

Ramblers' Association
1/5 Wandsworth Road, London SW8 2XX
Tel. 0171-582 6878

Calderdale Countryside Service
Leisure Services Dept, Wellesley Park, Halifax HX2 0AY
Tel. 01422-359454

Youth Hostels Association
Trevelyan House, St. Albans, Herts AL1 2DY
Tel. 01727-55215

Tourist Information
Piece Hall **Halifax** West Yorkshire HX1 1RE
Tel. 01422-368725

1 Bridge Gate **Hebden Bridge** West Yorkshire HX7 8EX
Tel. 01422-843831

15 Burnley Road **Todmorden** Lancashire OL14 7BU
Tel. 01706-818181

Information also at 40 Town Hall Street **Sowerby Bridge**
Tel. 01422-832564   (Saturdays and Bank Holidays)

The National Trust (Regional Office)
27 Tadcaster Road, York YO2 2QG
Tel. 01904-702021

Public Transport enquiries
Yorkshire Rider, Skircoat Road, Halifax HX1 2RF
Tel. 01422-364467

Pennine Heritage
The Birchcliffe Centre, Hebden Bridge HX7 8DG
Tel. 01422-844450

South Pennines Packhorse Trails Trust
The Barn, Mankinholes, Todmorden OL14 6HR
Tel. 01706-815598

LOG OF THE WALKS

WALK	DATE	NOTES
1		
2		
3		
4		
5		
6		
7		
8		
9		
10		
11		
12		
13		
14		
15		
16		
17		
18		
19		
20		
21		
22		
23		
24		
25		

INDEX

Principal features: walk number refers

96